WINNING THE FIGHT

WINNING THE FIGHT

A GUIDE TO PROTECT CAR DEALERS

STEVE LEVINE

WINNING THE FIGHT: A GUIDE TO PROTECT CAR DEALERS

Cover design by Shane Church
Book design by: Sue Balcer

ISBN 978-0-578-35463-7

Published by Ignite Consulting Partners
Fort Worth, Texas

Dedication

This book is dedicated to the best entrepreneurs in the world, car dealers, who continually amaze me with their ingenuity, creativity, resiliency and work ethic.

Contents

Foreword

November, 2021

My New York accent drastically changed the direction of my legal career. I was born on Long Island, New York, grew up there, went to college 20 minutes down the Long Island Expressway at Hofstra University, and never planned on leaving. Why would I? Family, great bagels, pizza, my sports teams, what more could I want? By the time I finished college, though, I took all of those things for granted and was tired of the cold weather, so when choosing a law school, I opted for sun and warm weather and attended SMU in Dallas.

To say me and my white IROC Camaro stood out is an understatement. I was My Cousin Vinny personified, and this was six years before the movie came out. My look, attitude, and life experiences made me a stranger in a strange land. As one professor summed it up, I was a pushy aggressive New Yorker. In Moot Court during my first year I wore a dark double breasted pinstripe suit and accented it with an emerald tie. One of the judges admonished me, saying that in Dallas serious lawyers don't wear ties like that. Ten years later every lawyer in Dallas dressed like that, but that's sour grapes for another time.

I never thrived, but somehow survived law school. In the summers, I clerked for an old, established Dallas law firm and was hired as an associate. When I showed up in September for my first official day of work, I was told the firm was disbanding and I had no job. This was during the financial crisis of the late 80's, so jobs were scarce. I jumped around a small firm or two and, fast forward a few years, I was a young associate or "baby lawyer" at a mid-sized firm in Arlington, Texas, which is halfway between metropolitan, supposedly cosmopolitan Dallas and the folksy "West" that began in Fort Worth. How I got that job is a mystery, since I didn't have great law school grades and hadn't achieved notable success at my other jobs.

From day one with the firm, I was lost in the shuffle. Nobody knew what to do with me. I was interviewed and hired by the firm's business and transactions department and I thought I'd be drafting contracts and learning how to work on big corporate deals, but when I showed up for work the first day it turned out that department had filled the position with another lawyer, one that actually had an impressive resume and career achievements. I truly believe they forgot they hired me.

I was awkwardly walked from office to office and was introduced to many of the partners, none of whom showed an interest in my pubescent legal skills. I wound up being assigned to a senior associate in the litigation department. I guess someone took pity on me. I was even given an "office", which had been used as a storage room in the basement. I'm serious! About the only benefit to this space was that the office held boxes of VHS cassette movies that were sequestered as part of a shareholder dispute involving a video rental business. I took the time to inventory the movies and gained some degree of popularity with the lawyers and staff by "renting" them out on weekends.

Litigation? Lawsuits? Trials? I had never shown the least bit of interest in this kind of work. I didn't participate in the mock trial program in law school and I didn't fancy myself a young Perry Mason or even Matlock; heck, I didn't even watch those shows growing up. Yet here I was, learning how to draft lawsuit pleadings, ask and answer discovery, and even occasionally taking a minor deposition or covering a low level hearing to get my feet wet.

I was handed off from lawyer to lawyer for about a year. One month I'd be handling insurance defense work, the next I'd be working on a personal injury case or a business dispute. I felt like a nomad. Then one day one of the partners came frantically running into my office and changed my path by blurting out "YOU'RE FROM NEW YORK, COME WITH ME".

As we were walking to his car to go meet with a client, this partner, who was Texas born, raised and spoke with a thick twang, explained that he was representing a local used car dealer in a lawsuit against its landlord and that the client was originally from New York and had a thick accent he couldn't understand. It was truly a Tower of Babel situation, and I was going to serve as the interpreter. It turned out that the client and I both grew up on Long Island, about 20 minutes from each other, and hit it off right away. I was assigned to this case, and quickly became the point person.

Next thing I knew, this dealer was calling me anytime he received a demand letter or was sued by a customer, and given the fact that this dealer was located on the infamous Division Street in Arlington and this was the early 90's, those lawsuits came quite often. I handled so many cases I might as well have had my own parking spot at the courthouse. Pretty soon other dealers heard about me and my caseload grew even more. Then I became active in the local used car dealer association and started attending those meetings, and I began picking up clients in Dallas and surrounding areas. I was actually generating clients for the firm and started to think I may even be "partner material" one day.

Fate then intervened, because one of the other associates left to start his own practice and poached a well paying client. A combination of belt tightening and increased scrutiny of the remaining lawyers followed, and I was told that the firm didn't think that my growing car dealer clientele fit with their more serious image. My days with the firm were over, so in one weekend I found an office, bought some used furniture, had a sign made, and The Law Offices of Stephen E. Levine was formed.

I continued to build my auto finance practice, found that representing car dealers meant I was never short on good stories, became active in the National Auto Finance Association and met lots of folks that would help my career, went in-house and started a legal department at a finance company, then joined the legal department at a bank, then had my own practice again, and things came full circle when I joined AutoStar Solutions, which was a dealer management software for used car dealers and brought me back to my roots of working with them and learning the business from a technology perspective. All of those experiences culminated in helping to create Ignite Consulting Partners, which was formed to fill what I perceived to be the gap between the services that law firms provide to car dealers and finance companies and what these businesses really want and need to be able to understand their legal and compliance obligations and protect themselves.

Along the way, I found a way to combine my love for writing with my passion for auto finance law and began contributing articles to various publications. The Fort Worth Independent Car Dealer's Association gave me my start, back when its photocopied newsletter came in the mail every month, and Jack Tracey at NAF and Rick Sly at World of Special Finance magazine generously took a chance on a young, pushy aggressive ex-New Yorker and published some of my offerings. Several others have been kind enough to publish my materials, and I owe a special shout out to Andy Friedlander at NIADA and Nick Zulovich at Cherokee Media, both of whom have provided regular space to let me grace the fine pages of their publications and reach their audience.

Over the years, folks have been kind enough to tell me that they've enjoyed reading my articles. Those compliments have encouraged me, because once an article is sent off, I never really know whether or not I struck a chord with the reader unless they tell me. One day it occurred to me that I've covered a lot of different issues over the years and started reading some of my old content. I liked the way the pieces fit together to create a picture of how car finance compliance has both evolved yet stayed the same over the years. I thought it would be a worthwhile effort to gather these writings in one place, where they can be enjoyed with those that share my passion for the intersection between the used car business,compliance and law.

And to think, it all started because of my New York accent.

Acknowledgements

There are so many people to thank! Words can't do justice for the gratitude I owe to so many people that have helped me along the way and contributed to any success I have had. I'll inevitably leave someone out and regret it later, but I want to thank:

My Dad, who was my role model for a lawyer and who would encourage me in my young and struggling career by telling me "as long as you have a phone and a door, you've got a business".

Steve Burke, my first car finance client. "What a long strange trip it's been".

John Boundy, now it's all your fault.

Tom Hudson, Larry Young, Eric Johnson, Mark Edelman, Shaun Petersen, Bill Denius and other fantastic lawyers that have been friends and mentors over the years.

Allen Dobbins, for showing me the power of positivity and dreaming big.

To Rick Sly, Jack Tracey, Nick Zulovich and Andy Friedlander, who each encouraged my desire to write and gave me the forums to share my thoughts.

Richard Hudson, for joining me on this crazy Ignite journey and handling all things I'm not good at, like anything technology related.

The many teammates I've had along the way. You taught me the value of collaboration and the joy of working towards a common goal.

Many of my opposing counsel, who taught me many hard but valuable lessons.

My clients, who have trusted me to provide guidance and counsel to protect their business. I'm proud that many of you have become my friend.

Most of all, to everyone that's taken the time to read my articles and allowed me to share my thoughts.

CHAPTER ONE

My Journey from the Courthouse to Compliance

The early days of my career included some colorful cases and people. As noted, I was an "accidental" litigator and my "embryonic lawyer" experiences proved to be a great training ground for learning what can go wrong during a car finance transaction. As it turns out, these cases also gave me great material when I started writing articles. I've included a few of my favorites.

WHEN YOU GET A LEMON

Time to share a deep dark secret. When I was a young lawyer, just starting to figure things out in my own practice, I handled some lawsuits on behalf of consumers *against* car dealers. My thinking was twofold. First, I had a bit of an underdog mentality chip on my shoulder, and I figured that if the dealer wasn't smart enough to use me as their lawyer they were fair game. Secondly, I thought that by taking the "plaintiff's chair" in some cases it would help give me a more well rounded view of all of my cases and I would learn some tips to make me a better defense lawyer.

The Lemon Van

There was one case in particular that to this day I consider "the one that got away". A prospective client called to tell me about his ordeal purchasing a customized van to help transport his handicapped daughter. Almost as soon as he got it home he started having problems. The windshield leaked, the sliding side door wouldn't lock, and there were a whole host of other mechanical problems that prevented him from using the van. So far, I was interested, but only remotely.

Then he shared that when he brought the issues to the franchise dealer's attention, he was told that since the van was customized they wouldn't even look at it, hiding behind the "as-is" language despite the fact that the van clearly wasn't able to be used for its intended purpose. I was becoming more interested, but I wasn't sure whether I wanted to take the case.

Next, he then shared that to get the dealer's attention, he made a giant lemon out of paper mache, painted it bright yellow, attached it to the top of the van, and drove around the dealership, picketing. Instead of trying to help him, he said the dealership's employees would throw things at the van and curse at him as he drove by. "Do you have any witnesses, I asked?" "No, but I recorded it on videotape", he replied. Now I became very interested. To top it off, he then told me that the dealership repeatedly called his house and threatened and cursed at him. Imagine my reaction when he shared that they'd even left some of these messages on his answering machine and he'd send me the recordings. Sign him up!

To begin my representation, I did what any good plaintiff's lawyer would do, I asked to see all of his transaction paperwork, which led me to find a few other enticing causes of action to bring in the lawsuit, including a deficiency in the retail installment contract that I believed would give rise to a class action lawsuit because I suspected that it was a systematic error. By the time I finished drafting the demand letter, I was convinced that

I'd struck gold. This was one sexy case. I had a sympathetic client, a callous defendant with cruel behavior that was documented, and serious deceptive acts and practices claims, too. The icing on the lemon cake was that lurking class action that I was going to unveil when the time was right. I saw a pot of gold ahead if I handled the case correctly.

Not So Fast

I sued everyone connected to the van; the dealer, the conversion company, and the finance company that held the note. I was convinced that this was going to be a wonderful victory that would garner me media attention and earn me a reputation as a serious litigator, not to mention lead to a nice recovery for both my client and myself. As far as I was concerned, my carefully drafted pleadings were a work of art, and the mountain of discovery I served along with the lawsuit, put the defendants on notice that I meant business.

I can spend a few thousand words walking you through what happened next, but let's just say things didn't go as I'd hoped. The manufacturer took an interest in my lawsuit, as well as others that had been filed against the dealer by other consumers, and moved to revoke the dealer's franchise agreement and the dealership closed down. The conversion company, who was out of state, used the dual strategy of offering some decent settlement money while at the same time raising some procedural issues, which would have caused delay and complicated my strategy. The finance company holding the contract took advantage of these developments and simply played hardball. Long story short, we were ordered to mediation and my client was much more attracted to the settlement money that had been put on the table, which would allow him to purchase another van outright and still have some spending money left over to care for his daughter, rather than endure protracted litigation which would have dragged on a while. Both the settlement and attorney's fees I recovered were decent, but not the windfall of money or attention I had anticipated.

Lessons Learned

While things didn't go as well as I would have liked, I did learn quite a few things from the experience that I believe helped make me a better lawyer and to this day influence my strategic thinking when advising dealers and finance companies, and there are plenty of valuable lessons for dealers, too.

First, take an objective approach when analyzing a case. Don't just toss a demand letter in the trash, study the allegations and honestly evaluate whether there's risk. If this dealer had fairly considered the facts, it could have resolved things pretty quickly and cheaply. Instead, it endured a great deal of scrutiny from its manufacturer, spent a lot of money on attorney's fees, and didn't survive. It's an extreme example, to be sure, but I bet that dealer had regrets about not making the matter go away when it could have.

Next, every dealer needs to realize that once a plaintiff's lawyer gets involved, all bets are off the table. I wasn't just interested in seeing the videos and listening to the recordings that the customer mentioned, I wanted to analyze the entire transaction to see whether there were other claims. This happens all the time.

A lot of lawsuits begin when a consumer walks into their bankruptcy lawyers and says "I can't pay for my car and I need to file bankruptcy". These lawyers don't get rich off of simple bankruptcy cases, they make money by finding underlying claims that entitle them to recover attorney's fees and damages. It's vital to study your paperwork and find problems before the plaintiff's lawyer has the opportunity to do so.

Also, invest resources in training your staff. The inflammatory facts of this case were like a law school exam question from torts class. The culture at this dealership obviously left something to be desired. While these events happened decades ago, they pretty dramatically show what can happen when the inmates are left to run the asylum. I like to think that as an industry we've evolved past circumstances like this, but I have a hunch that even to this day, lots of plaintiff's lawyers would say differently and can share stories similar to mine.

Finally, there is a misconception many dealers have that good lawyers won't work for "free" and the consumer won't be able to find one to take their case. Decades of experience tell me this is wrong. There are lots of excellent attorneys that represent consumers and are passionate advocates for consumer protection. Many are willing to work on a contingency basis because the consumer protection statutes often allow for a successful plaintiff to recover attorney's fees, plus treble (triple) or punitive damages. Don't think that you've got the upper hand, the consumer can often find competent counsel to put them on an even playing field. In some ways, it's the dealer that is at a disadvantage because it will most likely have to pay their attorney each month, while the plaintiff's lawyer will wait until resolution for its recovery. This dynamic is often used by the plaintiff's lawyer to it's advantage. When I handled defense cases I was often told up front "we'll never settle", only to have the client reverse course after just a few months of incurring attorney's fees.

Remember this story next time you are faced with a complaint or demand letter. It's a lot more efficient (and cheaper) to admit a mistake and move on rather than roll the dice on litigation. Reduce your risk and move on. Plus, you never know who's going to show up on the other side of the table.

CONFESSIONS OF A RECOVERING TRIAL LAWYER

I came to be a compliance lawyer after spending the first several years of my career defending car dealers and finance companies in a myriad of colorful lawsuits. After seeing the damage that litigation can do to a small business, I had an epiphany that I wanted to help prevent dealers from getting sued rather than defend them after the fact. What I haven't shared with many of you previously, though, is that during this time I also handled a few lawsuits for consumers and sued a few dealers.

Since I'm not Catholic, that's as close to "forgive me Father for I have sinned" as I'll get. I'm not apologizing, I was young, hungry and had a chip on my shoulder. My philosophy was that if a dealer wasn't smart enough to use my services they were fair game, plus I reasoned that if I didn't take the cases someone else would. To this day, I'm grateful that I handled these cases because seeing the world from the other side of the aisle greatly improved my analytical abilities to defend similar cases.

I was thinking about a few of those cases recently when I was preparing a presentation on avoiding lawsuits for a group of dealers at a state convention. They provide some valuable insight into how cases develop and evolve, I'll share a few stories.

Collections Gone Wild

I'll start with a case that involved some pretty egregious facts surrounding a dealer's collection practices. A lady came to me because she had recently fallen behind on some payments on her car and that the BHPH dealer was calling her non-stop. When she shared the name of the company, my ears immediately perked up, because I'd tried to make this dealer a client and was dismissively and sternly told that they had everything in order and there was nothing I could possibly do for them.

Being young, hungry, with the aforementioned chip on my shoulder, I sure did remember that statement as she started telling me about the dozens of collection phone calls she'd receive every day from this dealer. When I asked what proof she had to back up her allegations, she told me she'd mail me proof. Imagine my surprise when I received a videotape (Betamax!) of her finger scrolling through her answering machine, minute by minute, hour by hour, with literally 40, 50 and even 60 calls to her house in a single day.

That case started out as a simple "wrongful debt collection" case based on the fact that so many calls a day would certainly classify as harassment under the Texas collection statute and violation of that statute would also classify as a deceptive trade practice, which opened the defendant up to attorney's fees and treble (triple) damages. By the time I looked through all of the paperwork, though, I threw in several more claims because the dealer's paperwork contained several egregious errors. There were incomplete forms, ones that had mathematical mistakes, and I thought that the dealer had sold her vastly over-inflated aftermarket products that provided illusory benefits in violation of state law. Foolishly, the dealer, stubborn as it was, refused a quick settlement and burned several thousands of dollars defending my discovery requests before agreeing to a settlement on the eve of depositions.

The Lemon Van

The next case I'll mention involved a conversion van a gentleman had recently purchased to provide transportation for his disabled daughter. Almost immediately, the van had significant mechanical problems that left him (and his daughter) without transportation. My client tried to work with the dealership but it refused his requests, relying on the "As-Is" language. Then he picketed the dealership, driving around the lot with a large yellow lemon affixed to the roof of the van. You've got to admire his creativity.

When he first called me, I almost didn't take the case because I thought the mounting of a giant lemon on the roof was surely an indication of a difficult client. I knew all too well that the quality of the person in the plaintiff's chair matters a great deal. I changed my mind, though, when he told me he had taken video footage of the dealership's employees "flipping him off" and throwing things at him as he drove by. Next he told me about the "spot the lemon van and get $ 500 off your purchase" campaign that the dealership flashed on its display sign on the roadway. What sealed the deal, though, was when he sent me a recording of numerous threatening messages that the dealership left on his answering machine.

The end result was that I sued the dealership and finance company (just like a good plaintiff's lawyer, I was looking for another pocket for recovery) for every claim I could think of for this conduct, plus I brought a class action for a disclosure error that I found when studying the contract because I was pretty sure if the dealer did it to this client it was a systematic error made repeatedly. Without going into details, the end result was a favorable financial settlement that enabled my client to acquire another, dependable means of transportation.

Even though this is an extreme case with several explosive facts, there are lessons that I think every dealer should remember when it comes to how plaintiff's lawyers evaluate a case. First, I found the gentleman's story to be very sympathetic. As someone with a disabled sister, I was empathetic to his experience and I thought that a judge and jury would be, too. Also, I thought that the combination of the dealership's employees mocking this person (which he was smart enough to video, thank you VHS) and making threatening calls made punitive damages likely. Finally, I thought the danger of a credible class action would bring the case to a head rather quickly, which it did. If nothing else is learned from this article, it's important to remember that class action lawsuits rarely start out that way, they usually start out involving a mechanical problem, as was the case here, that turns into a much more dangerous class action once a lawyer gets involved.

Turning Little Problems into Big Ones

Anyone see a pattern here? In both cases, little problems turned into larger problems for the dealer once a lawyer started digging his nose into the details. In both matters, the dealer made a big mistake in not admitting it had a problem quickly and resolving the case. Between my legal fees and their own lawyers, they each spent lots of money that didn't need to be spent if they had just honestly evaluated the case early on and made things right. This is a mistake that I've seen lots of dealers make over the years, and a point that I always stress in training dealers on defensive litigation tactics.

I'd like to think that egregious examples like these would no longer happen because of the emphasis the industry puts on education, complaint management, and other defensive tools, but I'm not enough of an optimist to put money on it. That's why when I first start working with a new dealer client, I emphasize the importance of putting key compliance blocks in place so that if it is attacked, I'll be able to discourage the Plaintiff's lawyer by demonstrating how this client is different from the stereotypical dealer. The key to doing this is to have demonstrable evidence to back up that claim, and that's why complaint management, policies and procedures, training, risk assessments, and spot audits are so valuable! An ounce of prevention is truly worth a pound of cure, so take steps before trouble strikes.

COMPLAINTS, SOCIAL MEDIA AND VOODOO SPELLS

One of the biggest differences I see in the auto sales and finance industry now as compared to the early years of my career is the power that social media currently places in the hands of the consumer. Let's compare the use of social media by consumers today with a few of my more colorful stories from "back in the day" that involved how customers voiced complaints.

The Picketing Customer

Okay, "complaint" doesn't quite adequately describe the situations I'm going to share. The first story involves one very hot and humid August day when a client called to ask for advice on how to handle a customer that was picketing his car lot. He proceeded to share that he sold this woman a car a few weeks prior and almost immediately, it started having mechanical issues to the point where it wouldn't run. He had attempted to fix the vehicle a few times but the engine light was still turning on and the customer didn't think the vehicle was safe to drive and wanted a different car. When my client refused her demand, she decided to picket his store.

Since this dealer was only a few blocks from my office, I decided to see what was going on for myself so I drove to the lot. Sure enough, as I pulled up I saw a rather large lady holding a sign that said "Don't Buy a Car Here". She was marching up and down the public sidewalk, sweating profusely because she was in Texas and this was in August. My first thought was "oh my gosh, she's going to pass out, hit her head, and then sue my client". I went inside, grabbed a few cold bottles of water and a folding chair and went to speak with her. My client was livid with me, but I explained my concerns and calmed him down.

I offered this lady the cold water and chair and she looked at me warily. I asked if we could chat and at first she turned her back and marched away. I explained that I'd like to help get the situation resolved and she stopped walking, still skeptical but willing to listen. I asked her to tell me her side of the story. I should mention that I'd been trained as a mediator and one of the first things I learned in "mediator school" is that people need to ventilate and get their feelings out before a solution can be reached. So I invited her to share her frustrations.

She went on for several minutes, emotionally telling me how she had saved her money for a down payment for six months and needed reliable transportation because hers was the only car in her family. She shared that the mechanical issues she experienced had caused her to be late to work twice and that she was on final warning and close to being fired. She expressed fear that she wouldn't be able to pay for repairs once her limited warranty ran out the following week and that she'd lose her job.

Armed with all of this information, I went back in to talk to my client and practice a little "shuttle diplomacy". It took a bit of back and forth, but over the course of the next hour or two I gradually convinced her to come inside and talk, similarly convinced my client to have a dialogue with her, where everyone agreed that a repossession was the last thing anyone wanted, and the three of us worked out a resolution that satisfied them both.

The "Voodoo" Lady

The next case that comes to mind involved a lawsuit filed by a lady that was similarly unhappy with her vehicle purchase. Fortunately she didn't picket, but she did file suit. At first she had a lawyer representing her but by the time we met face to face during mediation of the case, she'd gone through two lawyers and was now representing herself pro se. Defending a case involving a pro se litigant is tricky, because the judges will often give that party a lot of leeway and relax the procedural rules. This was a "he said she said" case that I wanted to settle, but my client felt differently. He believed that without a lawyer representing her she was at a big disadvantage and wanted to continue the fight.

The mediator did his best to get things resolved. He pleaded, begged and cajoled both parties but to no avail. The plaintiff and dealer just weren't on the same page and there was no opportunity to bridge the gap. After a few hours of negotiations, where my client and I were in one room and she was in another, with the mediator going back and forth, he declared we'd reached an impasse.

We packed up our things and made our way to the front lobby, where we ran into the plaintiff, who was also leaving. She was distraught from the stressful day, eyed us angrily, and proceeded to wave her arms as she chanted words we couldn't decipher. She made quite a production out of it, while we just looked at her puzzled. Satisfied with her accomplishment, she turned and walked out the door. My client and I just looked at each other, wondering what that was all about. The receptionist, who witnessed the scene, informed us that she was raised in Cajun country in Louisiana and that the lady had put a voodoo spell on us. Great, as if I needed to be walking around with that kind of bad luck.

Which Brings Me to Social Media

"What does this all have to do with social media", you may ask? Everything! Back then, an irate customer could do what these folks did and resort to picketing and spells. They could also go file a complaint with the Better Business Bureau, which was a popular tool, or complain to a regulator I suppose, but I don't recall having to deal with many of those at that time. As a last resort, they could file a lawsuit.

The internet and social media have changed everything and given the consumer a lot more power. At first, there were websites that consumers would go to with complaints against a business. "Rip Off Report" and "Bad Business Bureau" were two sites I could recall. I'd actually go to search on them on a fairly regular basis to see what was being said about my clients. There, the consumer would tell their story and try to stimulate some support against the business. These websites, similar to the Better Business Bureau, would inform the business of the complaint and seek to get paid by the business to get things resolved. This was popular for several years, but has lost momentum with the rise of social media.

After all, a consumer doesn't need a third party when they can do the work themselves. Just one post can be seen by countless people and impact the business in question. Facebook and other social media sites have evened the odds, or perhaps even tipped them in the consumer's favor, because just about every business has a website and looks to gain the benefit of positive reviews. The consumers now use these same sites to post negative experiences and reviews and seek to reach "viral" status, where tens of thousands of people see the bad publicity. I was once called by a dealer that had had an online video complaint made by an irate customer go viral, with almost 100,000 views. In reading the reviews, in addition to comments from locals, there were attacks coming from all over the world. The genie was already out of the bottle and I couldn't offer much in the way of help.

Would the customer that picketed even waste her time today? I doubt it, I think she'd be more inclined to tell her story online and hope to corner the dealer into a settlement by creating a groundswell of support from other consumers in her area. Would the "voodoo lady" have bothered to go to the courthouse, or would she have been better off spending her energies voicing her dissatisfaction on social media?

Conclusions.

I think every small business today needs a plan to deal with social media reviews, both good and bad. Heck, there are plenty of companies out there that will manage the social media process for you and highlight good complaints and manage the bad ones. Managing your social media presence should be part of your overall strategy, and invest energy in complaint management too. The power is in the hands of the consumers, so pay attention to these issues.

MAY IT PLEASE THE COURT

During the early years of my practice, I had two main clusters of clients. One was dealers operating on the notorious Division Street in Arlington, which had earned an almost "anything goes" reputation and was pretty dependable to generate colorful cases. The other was in Dallas, on Buckner Boulevard. I had attended a few local dealer meetings, hit off with a few of the "regulars", and was able to turn a few into clients. The dealers in this area were a tight knit group, so as I had some successful case outcomes the word spread and I gained a few more clients.

The problem with having a concentration of clients in areas like this is that I often landed in the same courts and in front of the same judges. There was one point in time when there was seemingly a wave of lawsuits against some of my dealers, and I wound up in front of the same judge frequently in a very short period of time. To make matters worse, each of the cases involved similar fact patterns of significant mechanical problems that occurred right after sale.

These cases were brought in small claims court, so there wasn't a lot of discovery or procedural motions, it was pretty much show up and argue your case. Things came to a head one day in a case involving a very well spoken and articulate lady that had sued my client. She sympathetically made her arguments to the judge and handled my efforts at cross examination quite well. Once she was done presenting her argument it was my turn.

As every lawyer is taught in law school, the first thing you do when addressing any Court is to say "May It Please the Court", and then proceed with the presentation. So that's what I did.

"May It Please the Court", I began. Before I could get another word out, the Judge looked over the bench at me and through clenched teeth admonished me. "The Court is not at all pleased, Mr. Levine. Approach the bench". Uh Oh!

I did as I was told and the Judge promptly layed into me, telling me that I'd been in front of him one too many times, the cases all sounded alike, and me and my clients were wasting his time as well as that of the plaintiffs and juries. He reprimanded me to tell my clients to do things differently and stop encouraging lawsuits. He also advised that in the future, I was not allowed to show up in his court with a corporate representative acting on behalf of the dealer, as I had in this case. "The only person I want to see is the person whose name is on the sign", he commanded. He then said we were going to take a short recess and his expectation was that this matter would be resolved. His meaning was clear. My client had better get the matter settled and make amends with this lady. Although I didn't like the "gun to the head" approach, I did appreciate the opportunity to get the parties to work things out rather than having him simply rule against us, which was the direction things were going. Luckily, the plaintiff didn't shoot for the moon and we were able to tell the judge that we'd reach a resolution.

I immediately drove over to this client's store to share both the outcome and the judge's demeanor. Since this problem wasn't limited to just one dealer, I made a few other stops up and down Buckner, telling each dealer the same thing, which was that the judge was tired of hearing these cases and that if I had to go back in front of him, his explicit instruction was to bring the owner of the dealership with me. Now that statement got their attention;

they certainly weren't keen on having to face the music, that's what they paid me for.

What happened next was development of some of the best complaint management practices I've seen, and this was about 15 years before the CFPB emphasized the importance and made it an industry "must ". I organized a lunch for these dealers and as a group we discussed why these lawsuits were happening. What I learned was that they psychologically lumped all complaints into one big pile, and they didn't really put any effort into resolving them, figuring that most customers wouldn't sue and they'd weed themselves out and then they'd deal with the ones that did. They all admitted that they had personnel that felt it was their job to protect the dealership, not resolve the issue, and that oftentimes the dealings were acrimonious. We all agreed that this strategy was no longer working very well and change was needed.

Once the root cause was identified, we discussed how they could resolve complaints with customers early in the process, the importance of better communication within the businesses, how to work with the customers in a non-adverserial fashion, and how to improve the overall customer experience. A few of the more invested ones even held some of the resistant ones accountable and argued this was a threat to all of their livelihoods. These folks certainly seemed to get the judge's message, but the proof would only come over time.

The group's focus was a success, so much so that when I hadn't seen any new cases in a while I began to wonder if they'd found a new lawyer. I made a few calls and learned that no, they still considered me their lawyer, they just hadn't needed me because they were getting things worked out with their customers. A few even shared that they thought the overall mood of their team was better, and they certainly didn't miss the legal fees.

I'm happy to say that I didn't need to appear before that judge for quite a while, and when I did there was no mention of the previous case. I actually regret not saying something to him, because I did feel that his challenge had a favorable impact on my clients' business, though it did certainly adversely affect my income. As a young lawyer, though, I still thought of judges as omnipotent and was several years away from seeing them as people with whom I could converse.

So what's my "take-away"? Don't wait for a judge or regulator to be the stimulus for change. Every business should take a look at its customer satisfaction practices and continually strive for improvement. Ask the hard questions and objectively look at your business through the eyes of the customer. Do this and you will reap the rewards.

LESSONS FROM BANKRUPTCY COURT

An unintended byproduct of my representation of lenders was that sometimes I had to meander into bankruptcy court. I was going to say "unfortunate" instead of "unintended", because I never set out to be a bankruptcy or creditor's rights lawyer and never enjoyed it. I must admit, however, that there were plenty of lean months when the bankruptcy work I handled put food on the table and kept the lights on, so I'm thankful to have had the opportunity to learn those skills and provide that service.

Bankruptcy Litigation

My first experiences in bankruptcy court were defending finance companies and banks that had repossessed their collateral and then found out the customer had later filed for bankruptcy protection. Often, the customer didn't have insurance on the vehicle and my clients refused to give back the vehicle, so the consumer's bankruptcy lawyer would move Sanctions for Violating the Automatic Stay. Those were often sticky cases, and it didn't take me too long to learn which judges were overly sympathetic towards the bankruptcy debtor.

I taught my clients to file Motions for Relief From Stay, where we would argue that the bankruptcy stay should be lifted because of lack of insurance, failure to make plan payments, or some other reason. It wasn't the most glorious work, but it did teach me some valuable skills and I got to learn about a whole world that was previously foreign to me.

Things I Learned Along the Way: Do Something

The first thing I learned, and it shocked me, was that many lenders wouldn't do anything when they received a notice of bankruptcy filing. Those accounts were put into a separate queue, often never to be heard from or thought about again. What a lost opportunity and waste of money. There were certainly ways to protect your claim while spending limited amounts of money, and if you didn't want to do that, there was a secondary market to purchase these accounts. The price was a lot lower than the amount then owed, but that's a whole lot better than getting nothing.

The Importance of the Creditor's Meeting

Next, I learned that the bankruptcy Gods (Congress) had given creditors a gift called the Creditor's Meeting. At these proceedings, the bankruptcy trustee, as well as any creditor, could ask the debtor questions which were answered under oath. In my eyes, this was a great windfall. You didn't have to send notice of a deposition, you didn't have to let the debtor's attorney know what you were going to ask in advance, and you could learn just about everything you needed to know about the debtor and potential actions you could take to protect your client. Plus, this could be done cheaply.

I'd often be the only creditor's representative that showed up to the Creditor's Meeting docket. I don't just mean my case, I mean the entire docket, which may consist of 50 or more cases on a given day. To this day, I always advise clients to let me teach one of their personnel how to conduct questioning at a Creditor's Meeting, because it's essentially free discovery and is valuable to your case. Plus, your folks will get to know the debtor's attorneys and a lot of courtesies can be achieved without frivolously spending money.

Lots of Money Gets Wasted

Next, I learned that creditors often end up needlessly wasting a lot of money in bankruptcy court. Some will file a Motion to Lift Stay on EVERY case that comes their way, their intent being to get debtor's counsel to compromise to an Agreed Order Lifting the Stay if payments weren't made or insurance wasn't kept. While these Agreed Orders are very valuable because the creditor can then repossess the vehicle with no further action needed, I think they are often used excessively, given the fact that so many bankruptcy cases get dismissed in a short time after filing. My perception is that this practice has diminished over time, as creditors and their in-house lawyers have learned how to focus on efficiency and reduce costs.

Where the Money's At

Next, I learned that debtor's attorneys don't make a lot of money handling the actual bankruptcy cases themselves. The fees are very often controlled by the judges, so volume is the name of the game to make a comfortable living doing this type of work. That explains why you see so many bankruptcy lawyer advertisements.

What debtor's leeches (I mean lawyers) do to supplement this income, though, is to meticulously study all of the debtors contracts, demand letters, credit reports, and any other records, all in an attempt to find a mistake that gives rise to a cause of action that the leech/lawyer can bring as an adversary proceeding, which is a lawsuit in bankruptcy court. I teach my clients that this is why so many lawsuits, and even class action lawsuits, begin with a bankruptcy consultation. The bankruptcy attorney wants to see everything, and on occasion the prospective debtor may be better off staying out of bankruptcy and filing a lawsuit against the creditor instead in order to control the case rather than leaving it up to the Trustee for the estate to act in the debtor's best interest.

A Good Creditor's Lawyer is a Valuable Ally

If I'm going to grade myself honestly, I was merely adequate in my representation of creditors in bankruptcy court, I wasn't a powerhouse by any means. I had my litigation background to rely on, and I had collected the requisite forms over time, but bankruptcy wasn't the focal point of my practice. I never spent the majority of my time doing this kind of work which means I didn't know the judges and their habits and preferences, and I certainly couldn't quote the Bankruptcy Code Chapter and Verse, which means that I was at a disadvantage against most debtor's attorneys, who almost universally sleep with the Code under their pillow.

Today, I advise all of my clients to identify a bankruptcy lawyer in their area that is qualified to provide guidance should the need arise. You don't have to have them on retainer, but know who they are and perhaps even interview them before you need them, so they are somewhat familiar with you and your business and aren't starting from scratch in the middle of an emergency. Bankruptcy deadlines can be fast, so the worst time to look for a lawyer is when you urgently need one. Do your homework in advance, learn who in your area handles creditor's rights, and ask them questions about how the common matters are resolved in your area. You'll be glad you did.

FROM COURTHOUSE TO COMPLIANCE: AND YOU MAY ASK YOURSELF, "MY GOD, HOW DID I GET HERE?"

As regular readers know, I took a bit of an odd career path to get to my current role of preaching car finance compliance to my adoring flock (tongue firmly in cheek). In my experience, most compliance attorneys start off doing research, analysis, and similar endeavors. Once they've established they possess the requisite level of attention to detail, they make their way to actual client contact and seeing more of the "big picture". This development path contributes to why so many compliance folks take what I view as an "academic" approach to analysis of any particular issue.

I, on the other hand, accidentally stumbled into the litigation world as a young lawyer and my introduction to car finance law was defending dealers and finance companies in a tumultuous storm of lawsuits. My docket in those years was made up of cases involving wrongful repossessions, collection disputes, deceptive trade practices claims, and breach of consumer protection laws. I cut my teeth by preparing every case as if it would go to trial, which meant analyzing how the law fit the case and uncovering every fact I could to gain an advantage for my client.

Compliance wasn't a buzzword for me back then, much less a career path. For several years I worked my way up the food chain, case by case, becoming progressively more comfortable and better in my handling of these matters. I found a lot of similarities in my cases, and over time I started to become more familiar with the statutes and best defenses and felt I had an advantage over many of the plaintiff lawyers I'd encounter. There weren't quite as many "consumer protection lawyers" back then as there are today, so I felt I had a superior understanding of the playing field over an attorney that was handling a landlord case one day, a slip and fall the next, and then a car transaction case.

Over time, though, my career satisfaction diminished. There were a few reasons for this. First, let's face it, litigation is by nature acrimonious, and I'm not a conflict driven person. This was the era of "Rambo" litigation, where opposing counsel would pull out all of the stops. I came to dread Friday afternoons, which is when many lawyers would launch an ambush in the form of discovery or an emergency motion, just in time to spoil my weekend.

Secondly, the risks a lawsuit presented to my clients increased as I was tasked with handling more serious cases. There were times when clients confided in me that the case I was responsible for was a "bet the company" matter that could drive them out of business if we lost. Finally, to be quite candid, I was growing tired of seeing my clients repeatedly getting sued and then taking their frustration out on me for having to incur legal fees.

I remember being in court for one case in particular, when my client, usually filled with bravado, appeared visibly shaken and expressed concerns that losing the case would harm his ability to send his children to college. That was a heavy conversation, real life hitting you upside the head! It wasn't that specific case, more like a culmination of many similar situations, but around that time I had an epiphany and found myself wondering "wouldn't it be great if I could stop my clients from getting sued".

It wasn't like one day I woke up and decided to become a compliance lawyer. But just by having tht thought, I changed my efforts on behalf of my clients. I found myself using all of the lessons I'd learned in lawsuits to try to change the way they did things so they could avoid being sued. Rather than exclusively focusing on the lawsuit at hand, I'd also delve into what led to it and whether things could be changed that would reduce the likelihood of future problems.

For instance, if a client was getting sued often for alleged deceptive trade practices violations, I'd examine their process and paperwork and try to build in some defenses that would help with a defense in the event there was a lawsuit. I took many of the attacks I'd seen made on the collection side and created and conducted training to teach collectors what behaviors were magnets for litigation. I attacked many of the closing documents my clients used and eliminated troublesome forms and replaced them with ones that would provide better protection.

Over the course of a few years, I switched from litigation and spent more time developing strategies to help avoid lawsuits. I even remember going to an industry conference and meeting some other lawyers that had similar practices and it dawned on me for the first time that what I was doing could be termed compliance. As I made this switch, I stopped handling litigation altogether, because I firmly believe that you are either a litigator or you're not, and that it's very hard to switch gears on an hourly or daily basis. The mindset is just too different. That may not be true for everyone, but it was for me.

Sometimes people try to pigeon-hole me as a "compliance lawyer", but I reject that limitation. I view myself more of a risk identifier and business protection advocate. I examine a client's operations and the tools they have in place and look for ways to discourage plaintiff lawyers and regulators from making them a target. I find it to be like writing or directing a play or movie. I put the pieces together for my client so that if challenged, its story can be told the way I'd like it to be told.

I'm proud to be a zealous advocate on behalf of my clients and the car finance industry. Thanks to all of my clients who have shown faith in me over the years and allowed me to support them in their efforts.

CHAPTER TWO

Protecting Your Business

During my years working in-house (in a company's legal department), I learned a valuable lesson; that the business world is divided into "RG's" and "NRG's". That's Revenue Generators and Non-Revenue Generators, for those of you that aren't familiar with "corporate speak". Revenue Generators bring in the money and are the stars, receiving salaries, bonuses and accolades to match. Unfortunately for me, lawyers are considered non-revenue generators, so the compensation and other perks tend to lag behind.

Why do I bring this up? What's all of this got to do with car dealers? I find a similar stratification when it comes to how car dealers choose to spend money. They'll gladly invest "make ready" money if they think it will lead to a better sale price and generate revenue. They'll dump lots of money into advertising to generate leads. If someone is selling search engine optimization at a conference, the dealers will swarm.

Spending on compliance? Now that's another story. I've encountered quite a bit of reluctance when encouraging dealers to invest their dollars on strong compliance functions because there isn't an obvious correlation to revenue. It's usually an urgent crisis that causes my phone to ring, and many folks aren't interested in taking the "an ounce of prevention is worth a pound of cure" approach to protect their business. This chapter's articles are a collection of ideas on how to protect the business *before* the wolves are at the door.

LAWSUITS ARE THE BIGGEST RISK!

While preparing for a jury trial when I was a young lawyer, I sought out the advice of a more experienced lawyer on how to get a fair and impartial jury for my car dealer client. The older attorney looked at me, shook his head, said "I don't think there is such a thing", and advised me to go ask my firm's senior partner. I hunted him down next and asked him the same question. He didn't offer any encouragement either, and suggested I seek counsel from a former long-time judge who had recently joined our firm.

I worked up the nerve to present this question to the intimidating ex-judge, who had been on the bench for about 30 years, and was known for his cantankerous demeanor. He glared at me dismissively and gruffly asked which court my case was in. Once I responded, he then asked where I parked my car when I appeared before that court. I was confused, not knowing what parking my car had to do with picking a fair jury, but I answered his question. Based on the information I provided, he pointed his finger at me and growled that once I parked my car on the day of trial, as I walked towards the granite stairway to get to the main entrance of the courthouse, I was going to pass right by a sculpture of a large brass bull that stood in front of the courthouse (no, I'm not making this up, it's a Texas thing). As I hung on to his every word, expecting wisdom and insight, he then declared that if that large brass bull came down off of his stand and walked around, then and only then is when I'd get a fair and impartial jury to hear a case against a car dealer.

I share this story because dealers in general and BHPH dealers in particular don't have an appreciation of the inherent risk that lawsuits present. Over the past few years the overwhelming attention of the industry has been focused on the CFPB, headline grabbing consent orders, and the increased activity of other state and federal regulators. While all of that information is certainly important, lawsuits still represent the greatest risk to most car dealers across the country. After all, the odds of being sued by customers and denied credit applicants are a whole lot higher than the CFPB showing up at the door of any given dealer, the Herbie's case notwithstanding.

The focus on this article, therefore, is borrowing from my experiences to highlight some of the best ways to identify, manage and mitigate litigation risk:

Choose the Right Lawyer:

Do not take the decision of legal representation for granted. Pay careful attention to a prospective lawyer's industry specific background and experience. Too often, folks just assume that the lawyer that handled their business start-up or looked over some contracts is also the right lawyer to defend them in a lawsuit. Very often that is a costly assumption. Instead, look for counsel that has subject matter expertise in handling consumer disputes and knows the business.

Lawsuits sometimes have some pretty tight deadlines, so you don't want to wait until the clock is ticking to begin the selection process. It's better to think ahead and learn which lawyers in your area represent car dealers and what kind of cases they handle. There are distinctions. Handling a case involving allegations of breach of contract or deceptive acts is a lot different than one based on unique interest calculation or usury violations. Find the right lawyer that's got a track record of success. Use this article as a motivator to ask yourself whether you are adequately "lawyered up" should the need arise.

Train your Team to Manage Customer Complaints:

In my experience, the leading cause of car dealer lawsuits is poor customer service, which is often due to a lack of training and unfamiliarity with all aspects of the business. Dealerships should provide complaint management training to all employees that interact with customers in any way. Employees need to learn how to objectively analyze facts and learn how to listen. Luckily, these are skills that can be taught.

Don't fall victim to the logic "if they can't make a payment then they can't afford a lawyer". This belief is wrong. There are plenty of consumer lawyers that will work on a contingency fee or are pretty confident that a case against a car dealer will generate attorney's fees. Knowing this, the smart dealer will make sure that its employees provide good customer service and know how to handle customer complaints.

A lot has been said about complaint management in the last few years due to the CFPB's mandate that compliant management be a part of a dealer's compliance management system. One of the most valuable aspects of complaint management is learning how to identify commonality of issues and using this information to proactively look for ways to alleviate the risk. This will not only cut down on lawsuits, it will make your business more efficient.

To create successful complaint management within an organization, it's got to be prioritized, and by that I mean make it a part of customer service from the first interview forward. Emphasize it with all employees throughout the organization, build metrics on customer satisfaction, and reward the term for its success in this area. These actions will diminish the risk of disgruntled customers seeking an attorney and creating costly litigation.

Evaluate your Inventory:

Seriously consider the condition of the vehicles you offer for sale. I estimate that at least 1/3 of the cases I defended involved serious mechanical defects within the first sixty days of sale. It's hard for a dealer to appear sympathetic to a jury when facing those facts. Never forget that the judge and jury are consumers too, and will likely put themselves in the position of the consumer.

Too many dealers rely on the "no warranty", "as-is", and numerous other dealer friendly documents that customers sign at closing. Sure, those documents give you something to argue about in court, but the mere fact that you're in a lawsuit means that you've already lost time dealing with lawyers and incurred costs of defense, not to mention the additional exposure of possibly having to pay damages. I know it's expensive to purchase better inventory or make repairs; however, consider that those costs are a lot more controllable and predictable than the dangers faced in litigation.

Examine Your Business for Risk:

Take an honest look at your business practices. Have you thrown caution to the wind in an effort to enhance profits? Are you aware of what types of cases are being brought against the industry in general and dealers in your city and state, in particular? The following are some of the more common types of claims against dealers:

Adverse action letters have become a popular target of lawsuits. Can you prove they are sent? Are the adverse actions reasons provided to the applicant sound and consistent? Is your process defensible if challenged?;

Do you charge the maximum interest rate allowed by law? If so, a simple mathematical error can be turned into a usury case because such mistake can cause you to charge interest in excess of the maximum rate;

Have you vetted the add-on products you sell and the practices of the companies that provide them? Are you comfortable that the benefits to the consumer are strong enough to withstand a plaintiff's argument that they were illusory and misleading?

Is there an outstanding recall on the vehicle being sold and has it been disclosed in writing and acknowledged in writing by the customer? These have always been dangerous but are becoming increasingly popular causes of action;

Ask whether your customer can afford the payment. Long before "ability to repay" became a battle cry of the CFPB, the theory was commonly used by plaintiff's lawyers alleging an abusive and deceptive practice;

Audit the dealer management system and your deal jackets at least once a year to make sure that documentation and calculations are consistent. Sometimes a dealer will add documents to its package, not realizing that a form is inconsistent with another already being used. Also, a dealer may change practices without communicating them to third party service providers such as a dealer management software provider, thereby creating an error;

Collections are a breeding ground of litigation. At least once a year all collection letters and other written communications to consumers should be audited. Also, be sure to have a strong policy manual for collections, and regularly train collectors on its content. Being able to demonstrate these facts can be the difference between a weak defense case and a strong one;

The level of scrutiny on accurate credit reporting has never been greater. Examine your process for reporting and identify troublesome fact patterns. Additionally, have a strong process for handling of customer credit reporting disputes and make sure there is adequate staffing and training;

There's nothing worse than losing money because your customer didn't make payments, therefore resulting in repossession, only to lose again when failure to carefully follow Article 9 of the Uniform Commercial Code results in legal liability. There are lots of traps in Article 9. Have a qualified lawyer examine your repossession process and the required letters, including the notice of deficiency balance letter, to make sure your dealership is in compliance.

While this list certainly isn't all-inclusive, it is a good place for a dealer to start evaluating its lawsuit preparedness. Ask questions about the processes in place for each of these areas. Ask the dealership's business leaders and even some employees about their knowledge of these issues. My hunch is that you'll find plenty of opportunities for improvement.

Conclusions.

Lawsuits still remain the biggest threat that dealerships face on a daily basis. Win or lose, the loss of employee efficiency and productivity can be crippling. The costs of defending even a simple allegation can far exceed the amount in controversy, and that's without factoring in statutory and contractual damages that may be available to the consumer to cover its attorneys' fees. The smart dealer will critically examine its policies, procedures and practices to determine weaknesses and then devote resources to strengthening them. As Chinese Military Strategist and General Sun Tzu said: "The general who wins the battle makes many calculations in his temple before the battle is fought".

WHAT TO DO WHEN THE LAW COMES KNOCKIN'

Over the years, I've been involved in a good many matters involving audits of a dealership or related finance company by state regulators. As states continue to look to grow revenue, I think it's reasonable to anticipate an increase in these audits. They can be costly and greatly impact your business, so I encourage you to take a thoughtful approach to this subject and to share it with your staff.

It used to be that regulators would show up at your doorstep unannounced. Now, though, for both efficiency and budgetary reasons, many regulators send advance notice of an in person audit and some even prefer to have dealer's scan and mail information and never venture on site. It is important that dealer's know how to effectively respond in each situation.

The Basics

In whatever form the audit takes, you can bet that the state regulator is going to ask for a combination of files that represent paid off accounts, current accounts, accounts which have been repossessed, and files where the applicant was denied credit. This often comes as a surprise to dealers, who tend to think only in terms of active accounts. I've come to discover, though, that regulators prefer to take a holistic approach when examining the overall compliance "health" of the dealership. As a result, they'll comb over adverse action letters to make sure they are sent and contain compliant information. Similarly, they will study both the repossessed and charged off accounts to make sure that relevant laws are being followed, such as compliance with UCC Article 9 disposition of collateral issues, title matters and attempts to collect a deficiency balance.

The Off-Site Audit

Taking the example of an off-site audit first, these usually start with the regulator sending a letter compelling the dealer to send a sample of files. For instance, they may request ten files from each of the following categories: paid off accounts, active accounts, repossessed accounts, and ten files where the applicant was declined for credit. If you're lucky enough to have a regulator choose this method, please breathe a deep sigh of relief, select the files and immediately send them to your lawyer or compliance professional for an audit of your own so you are aware of any issues that may be present and even choose different files, if necessary. I know of more than one dealership that forwarded files without taking this step and paid the consequences with a negative audit that required costly refunds. That is dangerous, cheap, lazy, and inexcusable.

A variation of a mail audit is that the regulator first requests names of one hundred files in each of the aforementioned categories and then randomly picks their sample size and tells you which files to send. If this is the case, you've lost your ability to choose the files, but even in this instance, you should have your files reviewed by a subject matter expert so that you are aware of any issues that may exist prior to the audit. You may even choose to take remedial action, where necessary, and advise the auditor of the issue up front in an effort to gain leniency and demonstrate eagerness to resolve the issue.

The On-Site Audit

If you aren't as lucky and are, instead, subject to state audits where the investigator shows up at your dealership, it isn't time to panic, though, because you will put into effect the plan that you will develop as a result of reading this article. Because you are proactive and prepared ahead of time, you will inquire about their technology and other needs so that they can perform their job efficiently and without disruption of your business.

In the likely event that the auditor will want access to your management system, you will provide them with temporary access in an area where you can observe them and be available to answer any questions. You will want to make sure this area is away from the bulk of your operations and that the investigator doesn't have the ability to do things like observe closings and hear collection conversations with customers. You want to give the auditor all the information they seek and only that information. I've actually seen instances where what started out as a routine audit got messy because the auditor was placed near the collections department and got to hear phone calls and witness confrontations with walk-in customers. Hiring Perry Mason himself won't be able to wipe away the potential damage of impressions gleaned from hours of such first-hand knowledge.

I know of an instance where a rather significant investigation was commenced because the auditor was allowed to interact with employees in the break-room and casually asked questions about the nature of the business practices that tipped off issues that were not apparent from a review of the files. In another matter, the regulator saw a bonus promotion the dealer was running having to do with the sale of ancillary products, which led to an investigation of how these products were positioned with buyers. This is why it's important to provide every employee with training on what is and isn't proper for an auditor to ask, what should and shouldn't be said, and the appropriate chain of command within the dealership that the auditor should be required to follow.

The Findings

In the event that the audit picks up some matters that require correction, fix them quickly and show that you are a good corporate citizen. If you believe the auditor is incorrect in its interpretation of an issue, use an experienced professional like a lawyer or accountant to help you state your case. This not only allows you to take advantage of their experience, but removes you from having to get directly confrontational with the auditor.

Contrary to some water cooler talk I've heard over the years, the regulator doesn't want to put honest folks trying to do the right thing out of business, and they do recognize that some of these laws are pretty complicated and inadvertent errors do happen. Believe it or not, individual auditors even differ on interpretations of laws and regulations. If an error is discovered, you definitely want to be able to demonstrate that you tried to comply with the law and the mistake wasn't the result of negligence or conscious indifference but was, instead, the result of misunderstanding of a complex issue subject to differing interpretations.

Don't Hide Behind the Results of Previous Audits

A word of caution about the results of previous audits: they usually have no value as precedent. By this I mean that just because an examiner overlooked or even missed an issue in their last audit, it doesn't mean that the regulator can't issue contrary findings in a later audit. I know this is frustrating to dealers, who feel that if they've been examined and received a clean bill of health, they should be able to rely on those findings. Don't damage your relationship with the regulator going forward by focusing on the past.

Also, accept the fact that examiners are not created equal. They bring with them different experiences and skill sets. A small finding that one examiner chose to overlook may represent a larger concern to another examiner. One examiner may give cursory attention to repossessions and charge offs, whereas another may make them a focal point of the audit. My advice is deal with the hand you're dealt.

Conclusions

If you follow these simple steps you can avoid a lot of the pitfalls that plague dealers and lead to less than satisfactory audits. Maintaining positive relations with your state regulator is very worthwhile and is within the grasp of every dealership. Good luck and thanks for reading. I'm always glad to receive feedback and suggestions for future articles.

A BAD DAY AT THE OFFICE

I recently had one of "those" miserable conversations that we lawyers and compliance folks dread. A dealer asked for my help in analyzing a lawsuit recently filed against his dealership. He dismissively glossed over the specific facts, not showing much concern, and summed things up by classifying it a "nuisance" case.

Not So Fast - this is a Class Action Lawsuit

When I studied the lawsuit papers, I just about fell out of my chair, immediately seeing this was no run of the mill lawsuit. This is a CLASS ACTION case being pursued by a plaintiff's firm that knows how to press the issue. They are already looking to examine dealership records to identify other similarly situated customers to add to the class. At best this case will cost a small fortune to defend and at worst it could put the dealer out of business.

I had to deliver the bad news. It's those kinds of conversations that knock the wind right out of me, they are brutal. I had to explain that if the allegations in the pleadings were accurate, there was no quick and easy way to get rid of this case. Forget about budgets, inventory planning, and the typical daily worries that dealers face. Survival mode hits very quickly and the most pressing question is how much will this cost? While that depends on a lot of variables, the real answer is it costs a lot more than anyone plans to spend and will take a lot of time and energy and be a big distraction for the business. A lot of other needs will have to be sacrificed because this is a "bet the company" problem.

To make matters worse, the dealer is not particularly large, doesn't sell and finance many cars, and has a small staff. It is not in a financial position to take on this added litigation expense. In fact, on the basis of a few conversations we've had in the past, I could argue that compliance and best practices weren't prioritized because the dealer took the "I'm too small, it can't happen to me" approach. Well it did happen, and it does every day, to dealers and other creditors all over the country. Administrations come and go, regulator priorities change over time, but lawsuits remain a constant threat and continue to be the biggest risk faced by an independent dealer.

That Won't Happen to Me

Does that refrain sound familiar? Are a lot of you readers shifting uncomfortably in your seats? Let me say it again. This is a small dealer, doesn't sell a lot of cars, has a small number of employees, and I'm sticking by my argument that it pushes compliance to the back of the line because it isn't sexy and doesn't move the "profit needle" on a monthly basis. Gosh, that describes a lot of independent dealers and other financial institutions Let's face it, improving search engine optimization or finding a way to close more deals is front and center on your collective minds, but the response to a conversation about compliance is like what happens at the beginning of the drum solo at most rock concerts, lots of folks head for the door for a bathroom or smoke break.

The Threat is Real

The threat is real, folks. In my opinion, too many of you are comfortable whistling in the dark, hoping that the boogie-man will pass you by. The reality is it only takes one mistake, one employee having a bad day, one failure to follow the right process, and everything that's been invested in your dealership is at risk. If the allegations in the lawsuit are true, the case I mention has a lot of "ones" that add up into a perfect storm. Allegedly, the culprits included lack of policies, failure to follow the ones that did exist, careless completion of forms, failure to use an arbitration clause, lack of complaint management, and servicing errors. Many of you will smugly think "that's not us", but how many of you are willing to put that to the test in the form of a risk assessment or "mock" audit?

I'm not writing this as a scare tactic and I'm not being alarmist. I'm writing it to illustrate how just about anyone reading this is susceptible to the same horrible fate.

Another Horror Story

Want another sad tale, as if one is necessary? There was a recent decision handed down by an appeals court in Texas where a judgment against a dealer for almost $ 100,000 was affirmed, and that doesn't include the expense of the dealer's own legal fees for taking the case to trial and then appealing the jury verdict against it. The actual damages were less than $ 10,000, but it was the plaintiff's lawyers fees that put the big dent in the dealer's pocket.

The worst part is that the case centered around the dealer's decision to repossess a vehicle because of lack of proof of insurance and the "he said-she said" allegations that followed, not to mention the dealer's insisting on the customer's payment of a $ 500.00 repossession fee before returning the vehicle, despite the fact that the dealer didn't incur such fee. Throw in lack of written, consistent procedures, lack of an arbitration clause, poor account notes, and what seems to be a stubborn unwillingness to admit a mistake, and we've got another in a long line of ugly court decisions that presents our industry in the worst light possible.

Honestly Evaluate Where You Stand on Compliance

I implore this audience to "OWN YOUR COMPLIANCE" and stop sweeping shortcomings under the rug. Do some self examination, or better yet, reach out to me and I'll give you a list of some good places to start looking. Honestly assess where you are and develop a plan for improvement. If you've got some customer complaints or attorney demand letters that are weighing you down, reach out to someone with expertise in how to evaluate these matters and see what the real danger is and if it's better to work something out and move on. Stop simply hoping you won't be the next headline; hope is not a strategy. Instead, take affirmative and powerful steps to stop "IT" from happening to you.

THE HARD LESSONS KEEP COMING

I'm discouraged, and that's not normal. I'm usually fired up when I write an article. The recent double whammy of news of the Wells Fargo CPI investigation, coupled with the CFPB's findings in its payment fees bulletin of July 31st, has got me down, though.

Many trainers, consultants, publications and others in our industry have done a good job of getting the word out about the importance of treating customers "right". To be fair, there are a lot of companies that have acted upon the message and taken steps to improve the transparency of their business practices and create a better customer experience. Unfortunately, though, there are still many folks that aren't acting upon the message.

The Wells Fargo CPI Mess

The Wells Fargo CPI news includes findings that it wrongfully placed collateral protection insurance (CPI) on hundreds of thousands of accounts. This is very troubling, as it has been a "best practice" for years for institutions of that size to have policies and procedures in place to make sure that CPI is only added to an account as a last resort and after notice has been provided to the customer. This news is damaging to our industry. Wells Fargo is a big name that has had several recently publicized instances of compliance lapses. Its conduct will be imputed to the entire industry, so expect a new round of regulator, news media and plaintiff lawyer scrutiny and attacks.

In anticipation, lenders need to get their house in order. Review and update policies and procedures so that customer notice and communication can be demonstrated. Be sure there is a process to provide customers with advance notice that records indicate insurance has lapsed and CPI will be added unless proof of insurance is provided. Think about providing an additional notice after a few months to provide another opportunity to the customer to take action. Also, be sure to tell the customers that CPI premiums will be refunded if the customer can provide proof that such insurance was in place during the time period in question, build a process to make sure this happens, and then conduct some audits to make sure that it does. Remember that CPI fees can have a big impact on customer balances and many do not have the ability to repay the additional premium, so consider the overall impact this will have on how a regulator looks at the business, not to mention the overall portfolio and whether there is an unintended consequence of driving up defaults.

CFPB Payments Fees Bulletin

Turning to the CFPB's Bulletin on Payment Fees, which took aim at how the availability of free payment channels is communicated to customers, the big takeaway is the importance of having transparent communication of available payment methods and any associated fees. In my view, this Bulletin is really about the CFPB's dislike of the charging of these fees, especially when the customer isn't adequately told about the availability of free alternatives. That's a good way to catch a regulator's attention.

Again, BE TRANSPARENT. Look at how this information is communicated with customers and make sure all of the options are being clearly communicated, the more often the better. From the welcome letter to the website to IVR and other recordings, the customer should be given a clear picture of how to pay and those methods with fees attached shouldn't be given priority above the free options.

Conclusion

Both of these issues once again illustrate the need for transparency in customer dealings. It's crucial to take a look at operations and practices through the eyes of the customer. Are they being provided with all of the pertinent information? Are there opportunities to increase both the clarity of the message and the frequency that it is provided, so that the customer has a thorough understanding of the financial consequences of their choices?

Looking at your business through the eyes of your consumers can be uncomfortable, but it's only by doing so that improvements can be made. Technology is making the world more transparent and our business has the added pressure of ever increasing regulator, news media and consumer scrutiny. Lenders need to learn this lesson and make changes accordingly, or else the hard lessons will keep on coming.

AN UNFORTUNATE SENSE OF DEJA VU

I recently had reason to recall two lawsuits I defended back in the early days of my career. They were almost identical cases, in that the plaintiff in each case had sued my car dealer client after a repossession based on claims surrounding my client's alleged failure to return personal property left in the vehicle. In one case the claim for personal property involved $ 10,000 of leather goods supposedly left in the vehicle's trunk (what a coincidence that the claim limits of small claims court at the time was $ 10,000.00) while the other case involved several thousands of dollars worth of home stereo equipment that was allegedly stolen from the inside of a truck after repossession. In each case, of course, my client had no knowledge of such personal property.

Back around that time, there was a little bit of a "wild west" element to trying small claims court cases. The cases went to trial quickly, with limited discovery, and the judges would bring in the first six jurors in the jury pool, ask a few questions to make sure the potential jurors were alive and unrelated to either party, and then swear them in. To make a long story short, I won one and lost one.

The plaintiff that alleged that his stereo equipment had gone missing was victorious, mostly because he was able to produce receipts showing the purchase of the equipment a few weeks prior to the repossession (I know, I know, what was he doing buying so much equipment but not making his car payment), while my client's defense was only based on his testimony that there was no such property in the vehicle when the repo driver brought the vehicle to his premises. It was classic "he said - she said" and the jury ruled against us.

The lady seeking damages for loss of the "leather goods" lost her case, never being able to prove that these goods ever existed and withering under my spectacular cross examination that focused on her illogical claim that she kept leather clothes in a hot trunk throughout the summer heat of Texas. Again, it was "he said - she said" and in this case the juror doubted her credibility.

Both of these cases came down to the believability of the plaintiffs because my clients were left trying to prove they didn't do something. Back then, nobody took pictures of vehicles after repossession and they certainly didn't keep an inventory of property or have written policies and procedures to train staff on the steps to take post repossession.

Like I said, I had reason to think about these cases recently when two new clients each contacted me seeking guidance on how to handle very similar claims. This time, though, the customers had complained to their respective state regulator and now the regulators were going over their post repossession process with a fine tooth comb. Unfortunately, these two clients were still doing things much the same way as the dealers involved in the first two cases I mentioned, because they didn't have much in the way of a process either. One matter is still ongoing, but in the other matter the state actually forced the dealer to enter into a consent decree which requires, among other things, the dealer to provide the customer with a written inventory for each repossession for the next five years *by certified mail.*

I bring up these cases to illustrate the importance of having a strong written process for all post repossession dealings. Why? Because the dealer has already lost once in having to repossess the vehicle, it really stinks if the dealer loses a second time incurring defense costs for a lawsuit or regulatory action that is a "he said - she said" battle because there's no evidence.

Instead, I urge my clients to have a written policy in place. It should describe who is responsible for inventorying personal property as well as the vehicle's condition (company personnel or the repossession agent), where the vehicle will be stored, how it will be protected, the taking of pictures to memorialize the vehicle's condition, the process for a customer to reclaim any personal property (free of charge), and steps taken pursuant to Article 9 of the UCC for the disposition of the vehicle.

Armed with the evidence created during this process, the dealer or finance company is in a much better position to defend itself because it will be able to demonstrate that this process is routinely followed. It's pretty compelling if file after file is produced that contains pictures and an inventory and makes it much more believable that if the creditor did it in all of these cases, that it was also done in the case at hand. That puts the burden of proof squarely on the shoulders of the customer.

Don't take the post repossession process for granted. Debtors in that position often seek bankruptcy advice, and those attorneys know to look for these sorts of issues. Those customers are also already desperate and are looking for any way to turn the tables. If you invest just a bit in a strong process and some training, you'll remove a whole lot of risk from the equation.

WAR STORIES

This month I'm going to share the story of how I learned the hard lesson that "everything you say can and will be used against you in a court of law". I did a presentation recently on the importance of compliant advertising and told this story. The audience responded favorably, so I think it is worth sharing again.

Regular readers of this column know that I often refer back to the first decade or so of my legal career when I had the crazy idea that I was a trial lawyer. I worked for a law firm filled with lawyers that fancied themselves as such, and since I was the youngest, I was at the bottom of the barrel and got to work on the cases that nobody else wanted. Thus was my introduction to working with car dealers and auto finance companies.

One of my early cases involved a vehicle that had a transmission problem. Although my client had only sold it less than two weeks before the transmission gave out, he insisted that "AS -IS means what it says" and refused to do any repairs or offer the customer back the down payment. Not surprisingly, a demand letter from the customer's lawyer arrived quickly, with threats of all sorts of nastiness. That didn't budge my client, though, who took the "we'll see you in court" approach despite objections from his young and well-intentioned counsel.

Long story short, we wound up trying the case, which other lawyers in my firm soon came to refer to as "the butt whooping". It was a lousy set of facts because there was no question that the transmission was in bad shape at the time of sale since my client had previously repossessed it from another customer that had complained about it. To make things worse, the plaintiff was a single mother, saved up six months for her down payment, and was very sympathetic. It also didn't help that the consumer's lawyer was a wonderful advocate and commanded the courtroom.

Oh, he was also really smart and had been trying consumer cases for decades. He knew he had a strong factual case, a compelling client, and a defendant that didn't want to settle. He wanted to get in front of a jury as soon as possible, so he didn't waste time with a lot of pre-trial discovery, and since my client didn't want to run up his own legal bill, we didn't either, much to my dismay. In the opening statement, he argued to the jury that "AS-IS " isn't a license to rob, cheat and steal from the public. There's a legal concept called a warranty of merchantability and fitness for a particular purpose, which he said was breached. As you can imagine, every juror put themselves in the position of the consumer and was nodding in agreement.

Next, my adversary did something I thought was really clever, and taught me a lot about how to build and try a case. I expected him to call his client as a witness first, so he could question her and walk the judge and jury through her story. Instead, he called my client as the first witness, and rather than focus on the vehicle at issue, he attacked years of advertising that my client had published. Ads that emphasized "we treat you like family", "we care about our community because we live here too" and "dependable transportation at a fair price" were introduced into evidence. The other lawyer relentlessly questioned my client on these statements and whether he truly meant them or just said them to get business. He built the foundation of his case on the perception of the dealership that my client promoted in the community over the years. Only after doing that did he turn his attention to the vehicle in question and the transmission issue. The juxtaposition was obvious.

Needless to say, it was not a good day to be a car dealer, or its lawyer. The plaintiff won and got awarded actual and treble damages, and some pretty stout attorney's fees. My client got a rather rude wake up call about how judges and juries view a sympathetic customer that got the short end of the stick.

Although it isn't a pleasant memory, I tell this story because I think it's important for dealers to realize that this can happen to you. The lessons haven't changed. What you say in your advertising does matter, perhaps even more so today because the rampant use of social media gives plaintiffs a lot more ground to cover and possibly use to its advantage. Statements you make can and will be used against you. Your business practices better match up pretty closely to the perception that you put out in the public, because you may one day have to defend yourself.

So what's a dealer to do? Take an honest look at your business from a compliance perspective and look at it through the consumer's eyes. Have a strong complaint management process and objectively evaluate complaints. Evaluate your advertising and social media content and make sure you can back up what you say. Listen to your customers, show you care, and take responsibility when something isn't right. If you receive a demand letter, look at the facts from both sides and ask your lawyer to evaluate your case. Remember, the best time to settle is early, before there are a lot of legal fees at risk.

"AS-IS" MAY NOT BE ENOUGH TO PROTECT A DEALER

The exchange started innocently enough. I was reading one of the many social media BHPH dealer pages that I follow and came across a post where a dealer was seeking advice. He had recently sold a vehicle that developed engine trouble soon after he sold it (the very next day) and had been dealing with an irate customer, who was now threatening to hire an attorney. Since he had sold the vehicle "As-Is", he believed the customer purchased the vehicle subject to all defects and was asking whether he had anything to worry about.

One after the other, fellow dealers weighed in and backed up this dealer's reliance on the "As-Is" nature of the sale. While I'm usually reluctant to get involved in matters like this and certainly don't want to be perceived as giving legal advice on social media or being a "know it all", I've handled several cases like this in my legal career, so I thought I'd be helpful and remind the members that many states have consumer protections called "an implied warranty of merchantability" and "fitness for a particular purpose", as well as deceptive acts and practices laws that provide consumers with a whole host of claims, such as making it a violation to sell a product that doesn't perform its intended purpose or failing to disclose information about a product at the time of sale. These nebulously worded statutes can be difficult and expensive for a dealer to overcome.

I should have known better. The responses were swift and somewhat hostile. I was accused of trying to stir up trouble and business. I was told by several folks that they'd been selling cars

"As-Is" for decades without an issue. It was even suggested that I turn in my law license, if I even had one (Texas Bar Number available upon request).

I hate to be the bearer of bad news, but I do stand by my guidance. "While "As-Is" sales do offer some degree of protection, it isn't an automatic "Get out of Jail Free" card. There are lots of ways for a consumer lawyer to defeat this defense. In addition to the ones I already pointed out, there's lots of other strategies depending upon the facts of the case and the course of dealings between the parties. Did the dealer advertise anything that can be used against it? Did the dealership promise anything to the customer? Did the dealer's paperwork or statements from personnel contain any representations that arguably contradict the "As-Is" nature of the sale?

The point is that lawsuits like this are time consuming and expensive, and there's no certainty of the outcome. The dealer can make a motion for summary judgment on the basis of the "As-Is" sale, but even that's expensive and can be defeated with some artfully written factual allegations. My best advice is to seek to resolve the customer's issue, if at all possible, rather than hope that the "As-Is" statement will hold up under judicial scrutiny. In the long run, it's cheaper and better for business. Now you may run into a plaintiff's attorney that makes this all but impossible, and in that case you have no choice left but to fight, but as a starting point I think it's smart to look at the applicable laws in your state and facts and be brutally honest about the case up front to better prepare a defense strategy.

I'm an advocate on behalf of the car sales and finance industry and I have proudly represented and worked with dealers for decades. I zealously work to further their interests. That doesn't mean that I'm going to sugar coat things and give folks a false sense of security. Dealers can count on me to give it to them straight and honestly, even when what I have to say isn't popular, and even when I risk incurring their wrath by playing Devil's Advocate.

BEWARE OF THE ADVICE YOU CHOOSE TO TAKE

My good friend and former boss Allen Dobbins used to lambast me for not playing "the lawyer card" enough. He thought I should remind people that I have a law degree when we were in the midst of a conversation and someone provided legal advice they weren't qualified to give. For instance, if we were on a conference call and someone would share their interpretation of a certain law without any expertise to back it up, he'd want me to say something like "what law school taught you that"? I've been called a pushy and aggressive ex-New Yorker plenty of times, but that's just not my style, so I came up with more tactful ways to handle those situations.

Recently, I had a cringe-worthy moment that reminded me of Allen's "lawyer card". A client was repeatedly resisting my advice on a particularly thorny issue based on a "legal opinion" that had been expressed years earlier by a person that had lots of industry experience and knowledge but no legal background. I knew my answer was correct and the advice they preferred to follow didn't take into account the nuances of this delicate legal issue. What's more, I knew that if my client continued to follow this faulty advice they'd eventually get in trouble.

After respectfully disagreeing and stating my position several times, frustration finally got the better of me and blurted out "did this advice come from a lawyer, because a complex issue like this requires more than a guess". I'm sure Allen would have smiled, but I truly disliked having to say it and had immediate regret. I may have made my point, but did my client interpret my response as being pompous?

I bring this up because I see variations of this happening a lot on Facebook industry pages, chatrooms, at industry meetings and so forth. I find it comes up a lot when I have an initial conversation with a prospective client and delve into their practices and operations. Allen used to jokingly say he was a self made "internet lawyer" because that's where he'd look for legal answers. I think there are a lot of "internet lawyers' out there, and a lot of folks are taking unknown risks as a result of following their advice.

I often read Facebook posts from groups where dealer's go to each other for guidance on a wide variety of issues. In one recent example, the subject had to do with a dealer's credit furnishing obligations in a complicated situation and there was no shortage of commentary. Unfortunately, the loudest voices didn't appear to have a grasp of the issue, and some dangerous advice was being given. Similarly, there was another post having to do with internet sales across state lines and the applicability of rate caps and other laws. Here too, there was no shortage of opinions, some pretty creative thinking, but no appreciation of the dangers lurking. Finally, a dealer asked for advice on post repossession UCC Article 9 letters and dealers from far and wide weighed in, with many not considering that many states have distinct requirements for these letters plus a whole other myriad of issues to consider like disposition of the collateral and whether a deficiency balance will be pursued.

Please don't interpret this to mean I don't support these groups. To be clear, I think they are wonderful and add tremendous value. I commend the dealers that participate and want to help their fellow dealers. I do want the participants to realize, though, that when it comes to compliance and legal advice, sometimes the adage "you get what you pay for" is very true. While it's great that everyone wants to share their opinions and help their fellow dealers, everyone needs to realize that what works for one person may not work for another.

I often speak to 20 groups and at other industry events, and I always make it a point to tell folks that my presentations are generalizations and they need to seek out their own qualified professional guidance if they've got a specific question. I do this because the correct answer often depends on the various state laws, the business model being followed, the preferences of a particular regulator, and even whether an issue is frequently litigated in certain states. What may be sound guidance in one state can be flat out wrong in another, and I think that this fact often gets overlooked.

To sum it up folks, while it's great to ask questions and learn a lot of different points of view, not all guidance is equal when it comes to legal and compliance matters, so choose your teachers carefully, consider the complexity of the issue, and maybe even ask yourself whether it's time to seek out an expert of your own.

EMBRACE TECHNOLOGY, BUT UNDERSTAND THE LEGAL RISKS

I've been working with car dealers and auto finance companies for about 30 years. That means I'm old enough to remember when the fax machine ruled the business and the worst thing that could happen was to run out of thermal paper. I even had a client by the name of One Hour Acceptance! Of course, thanks to newer technology, both one hour credit decisions and the fax machine have been reduced to the scrap heap of history, and new technologies have given rise to instant credit decisions, online sales and many other changes that have made the industry barely recognizable from just a few decades ago.

While the benefits of technology are wonderful, I'll let you all in on a not so little secret - the evolution of the law moves a lot slower than the development of new technologies and sometimes results in a sizable gap between what the ultimate user wants to accomplish and what the law will clearly allow. The examples are numerous, but in the interest of brevity I'll cover just a few of the more serious ones that come to mind.

The Sale and Delivery of Vehicles

Online credit applications, 360 degree virtual tours of vehicles, and e-contracting have made it possible for customers to purchase (and finance) vehicles without ever stepping foot on a car lot. This method picked up a lot of steam in the last 12-18 months as Covid related stay at home orders and local mandates required small businesses to learn on the fly to survive. Many dealers were able to survive because they adeptly used available technologies to direct their business away from in-person sales to internet based sales and remote delivery.

Sounds simple enough, right? Not so fast! Many states have strict rules about what constitutes a "remote" sale and whether one can take place away from the licensed location of the dealership. Some, but not all, recognized the challenges their licensees faced and suspended these rules on a temporary basis. However, as business is returning to normal and these changes are being retracted, dealers need to make sure they fully understand the rules in place and whether adjustments in their model will require new licensing or other accommodations.

E-Signature and E-Contracting

Legal treatises have been written on these subjects, but for the purposes of this article I'll stick to the basics. The important thing to understand is that e-contracting and e-signature are different. E-signature refers to the capturing of a mark or signature as evidence of consent or approval on a document. This is pretty simple and has become a fairly common tool. E-contracting is the digital creation, validation and execution of a contract. While it usually does include an e-signature, a lot more goes into the creation of a valid E-contract, such as the presentation of a digital contract, its storage, and the chain of custody to maintain the validity and enforceability of the contract. So far - so good, right? Again, not so fast.

In the haste to use technology to drive business in the face of the pandemic, many third party service providers seemingly blurred the lines between the two and developed E-signature platforms that dealers either believed or were led to believe resulted in the creation of an electronic contract. As a result, many dealers thought that they were originating electronic contracts but were instead merely obtaining an electronic signature. Some found this out the hard way when they tried to sell their originations and were rejected. Others ran into issues with their capital providers, who weren't advised of the change in process and took the position that it was a violation of loan covenants. The lesson to be learned is that the details matter a lot, and it's vital to fully understand the legal ramifications when switching to a new technology or process.

GPS and Starter-Interrupt Devices

These devices are another example of how innovation has greatly impacted the auto finance business. Many dealers and lenders won't put metal on the street without having the devices in use. Again, though, it's important to understand the laws that are in place and how they can be used. Many states don't specifically regulate the use of these devices, but general consumer protection laws, which do exist almost everywhere, make it prudent to fully disclose the existence of the device to the customer and obtain the customer's written consent to the placement and use of the device. Regulators care about the disclosures and want to make sure that customers are informed.

Further, the repossession process is governed by both state motor vehicle sales finance laws as well as Article 9 of the Uniform Commercial Code and many jurisdictions have taken the position that the use of a starter interrupt device to shut off a vehicle is a constructive repossession. Creditors are wise to follow the "right to cure" and other relevant laws. Those operating in several states (or even a company in one state that has customers travel into other states) have to understand the laws of multiple jurisdictions and how they can impact the collections and repossession process.

The Remote Workforce

Here again, the abundance of available tools provided dealers and finance companies with the flexibility to move quickly to a remote environment when stay at home orders threatened to scuttle business. Many have embraced the remote workforce and are keeping it in place in some form or fashion. While this has proven to be efficient and beneficial for many, it's important to investigate the details.

Does your state allow collectors or those fulfilling other servicing functions to work from home, or must they all be at a licensed location? If the performance of job duties remotely is allowed, are adequate steps being taken to protect customer information and keep proprietary business information secure? What controls have been put in place to manage this new process? Does your employee handbook and other human resources policies provide clear direction on remote workplace issues? Again, it's easy to embrace the efficiencies, but be sure to understand the many related issues.

Conclusions

As I said at the beginning of this article, the development of technology moves a lot faster than evolution of laws and regulations.

Sometimes the results can be frustrating and clear answers and legal opinions are impossible. While I'm a firm believer in "moving at the speed of business", it's important to conduct due diligence and understand where there is legal clarity and where there isn't. Auto dealers and finance companies are some of the greatest entrepreneurs around and will find ways to overcome obstacles, but in doing so they need to take a thoughtful approach, realistically understand the risks, and make informed decisions.

THE OPPOSITION'S PLAYBOOK

Every once in a while I like to do opposition research. The opposition I am referring to are the plaintiff's lawyers and consumer advocates that regularly sue car dealers, finance companies and others in the credit industry. Please understand, I'm not talking about the "run of the mill" lawyer that may every now and again sue a car dealer, I'm talking about highly successful, well funded plaintiff's firms that aggressively pursue these types of cases. It's an important distinction, because the litigation experience, costs and outcomes are very different when confronted by this opponent.

The research I mentioned is that I recently listened to a podcast hosted by some of these very successful lawyers. A few things immediately stuck out to me. First, they have been doing this a long time and are intricately familiar with how to use the statutes in their favor. Secondly, they zealously believe in what they do for a living and are passionate about wanting to protect consumers. Lastly, litigating against them would be expensive and time consuming.

The presenters made a few comments that I found particularly interesting. One said that he is very confident that he can find a statutory violation in any matter that a potential client comes to him for consultation. Whether it's a claim under the granular consumer protection statutes, or a more general claim under a deceptive trade practices type statute, he's going to find something and then it's just a matter of whether he thinks there are enough damages and compelling facts to hold his interest. The other presenter then chimed in and added that he's like a dentist, he looks at what's in front of him and may say "there's no cavity today, but I can tell there will be one in six months". He went on to explain that if he doesn't see or hear any interesting facts from the client, he'll suggest having the consumer mail a "do not call instruction", raise a credit dispute or some other issue, or forward to him all emails or texts received from the creditor, because very often a more obvious claim will appear out of those efforts.

So what's a well intentioned creditor or car dealer to do to protect itself? Here's a few recommendations:

First, make sure you have a robust complaint management process. What was true decades ago when I was going to court defending these cases is still true today.....every lawsuit starts out as a customer complaint. There is almost always an opportunity to resolve the matter early on in the process, so it's vital to objectively look at each complaint and act accordingly. It's important to be impartial, truly listen to the customer, and seek a creative solution. The biggest mistake I see folks make in this area (besides simply not having strong complaint management) is thinking they are always right. It's important to actively look for opportunities to get better and learn from your customers. Don't just dismiss what they say.

Next, make sure your team knows how to handle "do not call" instructions as well as credit disputes. These are two popular claims brought by plaintiff's lawyers, and very often they are used to set creditors up for a lawsuit. Make sure your process is strong and your team understands the risks.

Finally, plan your defense before bad things happen. By this I mean think about the story you want to be able to tell and the favorable light you want to be able to present your company in. Do you have written controls in place like policies and procedures? Is there a demonstrable training program that will impress a judge or jury that you are trying to conduct business the right way? Do you regularly audit certain touch points of the business to make sure things are functioning like they should? Areas like adverse action letters, "do not call" requests, repossession letters and disposition of collateral and call frequency are just a few ideas to check into on a regular basis.

There are lawyers out there that make a very good living praying upon creditors, so it's important to put some work in and get your defense house in order. While there's no such thing as compliance perfection, there are lots of steps that can be taken to protect your business. If you do these things, hopefully you'll be a less appealing target and the opposition will go pick on a more attractive target.

THE "OTHER" THREAT THAT KEEPS ME UP AT NIGHT

A lot's been written recently about the impact the Biden Administration will have on consumer protection and the coming wave of regulation it will bring to auto finance. Between new leadership at the Consumer Financial Protection Bureau ("CFPB"), similar agencies being created at the state level, and the increased scrutiny of lender practices that is sure to follow, there is certainly a lot to keep in mind; however, I want to make sure our audience is also aware of what I perceive as the other side of that "risk coin" to BHPH and independent dealers, and finance companies, and that's the lawsuit wave that I see just over the horizon.

The Coronavirus Crisis has Caused a Court Backlog

By the time this article makes it to circulation, the Coronavirus crisis will have been in existence for a year. During this time, it has had a drastic impact on our court system. Stay at home orders and rampant infections in some localities led to many courts being closed for months. Even after court personnel came back to work, there was a tremendous backlog of paperwork and procedural matters to deal with on existing cases.

Almost overnight, judges had to create rules for "virtual" hearings and the lawyers practicing in these courts had to adapt to a "new norm". There was so much emphasis on existing cases that, as a result, new filings have been dramatically reduced. As a practical matter, this means that a great many plaintiff's lawyers chose to stop filing lawsuits in 2020. One local lawyer I know shared with me that he had no incentive to file any new consumer cases while there was so much uncertainty. Several other attorneys that practice on each side of the docket have shared similar views.

The Sharks are Circling

I anticipate that's about to change, though, and filings will return with a vengeance. There are a lot of hungry lawyers out there that want to get back to work and need to start generating revenue. They want to get back in front of judges and juries and do what they do best. As the court's work through the backlog, and especially when courts begin having more live proceedings, you can expect the number of consumer lawsuits being filed to quickly rise.

It's important to understand that there are litigators and then there are trial lawyers. What I mean by that is there are a lot of lawyers that will file cases and quickly overwhelm the defendant with written discovery and motions, all with the goal of obtaining a quick settlement by making it obvious that the case can be resolved for less than the cost of the legal fees incurred in responding to their tactics. Distinct from these lawyers are a more select group, the true trial lawyers, who live to zealously advocate their client's position in front of a judge and jury.

I mention this because the vast majority of these trial lawyers haven't been able to try cases for the past year. My belief is that these attorneys will be anxious to get back in the courtroom and in front of sympathetic juries that themselves have lived through this health crisis, have suffered the hardships of reduced income and experienced their own struggles to pay bills, and will be scrutinizing the actions of creditors such as car dealers and finance companies to a heightened degree. More so than ever, juries will come to the jury box with a disposition to favor the consumer.

I encourage all of you to be mindful of the court situation in your own towns and counties. Is the case backlog shrinking, are new cases being filed, and perhaps most importantly, has the virus situation improved to the point where live proceedings are happening? Those will be the advance indicators to the filing of more consumer lawsuits.

Prepare Your Defenses Now

What can you do to prepare? First, make sure your personnel have a strong process for the handling of customer complaints. Every consumer lawsuit I ever defended started out as a complaint that was escalated due to non-resolution. In fact, the law books are filled with big dollar verdicts against car dealers that started out as minor matters that could have been resolved for small repairs or similar outcomes. Keep track of the complaints that come in, make sure your personnel have the tools to resolve them, and be proactive and look for common issues that repeatedly arise.

Next, have your deal documents examined by a compliance professional or attorney. You can bet that any attorney looking at a lawsuit against a dealer will pick apart the paperwork looking for additional causes of action? One powerful reason is because contract claims usually allow for the recovery of attorney's fees, while many other types of actions do not. We do a large number of document reviews and often find contradictions and inconsistencies between documents. Get yours examined and reduce that risk.

Another good strategy is to examine your collection tactics. Collection lawsuits against creditors are a natural by-product of a crisis. Do you have strong written policies in place? Do you provide regular training to your collection personnel (and all employees, for that matter), and do you issue scripts to be followed? If a creditor has to defend itself from alleged bad behavior, these controls can be the difference between a benign case or a dangerous one.

I've long preached the importance of using arbitration agreements in consumer transactions. Although the Democratic Party platform included a goal of limiting or doing away with them, for now they are enforceable and strongly recommended. They are a great defense against runaway judges and emotional juries, not to mention limits on class actions. If you are using one, then have it re-examined to make sure it's up to date based on the latest guidance from the courts.

Conclusion

While the new Biden Administration will undoubtedly usher in an era of increased regulatory scrutiny and new legislation to advance consumer protection, it's important to recognize the risk that exists closer to home in your local courthouse. The backlog that exists in our legal system won't last forever, and as more of the population gets vaccines and the rate of infections hopefully slows down, we can anticipate an aggressive wave of lawsuits against car dealers and creditors. Following the suggestions I've outlined is a good step in protecting your business, and as always, feel free to reach out if you'd like to discuss your given situation.

CHAPTER THREE

Meet the New Boss: The CFPB

The Consumer Financial Protection Bureau ("CFPB") opened its doors in July of 2011. It had a simple message for consumers: "We've got your Back". I was in my mid 40's at the time, and I remember talking with another car finance attorney and we both concluded that this new agency would keep us busy for the rest of our careers.

That premonition has proven to be true, and in the last ten years the Bureau has been the driving force for compliance initiatives within the industry. Compliance became more than a buzzword and in my opinion, there are many things about our industry that are better as a result. There have also been many things about the CFPB that I haven't liked, and I haven't been shy about sharing those opinions in my articles.

MEET THE NEW BOSS: THE CFPB'S IMPACT ON AUTO FINANCE

This article is different from all of the other articles found in this book. I wrote this paper as a companion for a presentation I was giving to the State Bar of Texas Consumer and Commercial Law Section at it's annual meeting in 2015. Talk about walking into the Lion's Den! This presentation was to a room full of plaintiff's lawyers. I'm including it here because I think it does a good job of bringing the reader up to speed with the impact the CFPB had on auto finance as of its writing.

I - Abstract:

Auto Finance companies and used car dealers that collect their own contracts face unprecedented scrutiny because of the Consumer Financial Protection Bureau's interest in protecting consumers. The past few years have brought a great deal of change to the industry and the rules are still being developed. Prudent plaintiff's lawyers should examine this changing dynamic and adjust their strategies accordingly.

II - Introduction:

The Consumer Financial Protection Bureau ("CFPB" or "the Bureau") was created by the Dodd-Frank Act in 2010. Richard Cordray, a former Ohio Attorney General, was appointed by President Obama as its first Director in January of 2012.

A. The Bureau's Purpose.

Its purpose is to seek to implement and, where applicable, enforce consumer financial law consistently for the purpose of ensuring that all consumers have access to such products and services and that the markets for them are fair, transparent and competitive.

B. It's Mandate.

Its mandate is to ensure that 1) consumers are provided with timely and understandable information to make responsible decisions; 2) consumers are protected from unfair, deceptive or abusive acts and practices and from discrimination; and 3) outdated, unnecessary, or unduly burdensome regulations are regularly identified and addressed in order to reduce unwarranted regulatory burdens; 4) federal consumer financial law is enforced consistently; and 5) markets for consumer financial products and services operate transparently and efficiently to facilitate access and innovation.

C. It's Primary Functions.

The Bureau's primary functions are to 1) conduct financial education programs; 2) collect, investigate and respond to consumer complaints; 3) collect, research, monitor and publish information relevant to the functioning of markets for consumer financial products and services to identify risks to consumers and the proper functioning of such markets; 4) supervise covered persons for compliance with Federal consumer financial law and take appropriate enforcement action to address violations of such laws; 5) issue rules, order and guidance for implementing Federal consumer financial law; and 6) perform support activities as may be necessary or useful to facilitate the other functions of the Bureau.

D. Article Focus.

It would be an understatement to say that the Bureau has been aggressive in its efforts to educate and protect consumers. The focus of this article will be to examine the impact it has had on auto finance, to introduce the consumer law practitioner to the issues faced by the auto finance industry, and illustrate the significant changes that have occurred these past few years. Please note that while car dealers are statutorily exempt from CFPB coverage, their activities are still subject to oversight because the finance paper generated through them is sold to both captive finance companies and independent finance companies that are subject to examination and supervision. Further, there is oversight over car dealers that hold their own paper, traditionally called "buy here – pay here" dealers.

E. Historical Perspective of Regulation.

Even prior to the creation of the CFPB, the auto finance industry was subject to a myriad of applicable laws. Some, like Uniform Deceptive Acts and Practices ("UDAP") statutes, focused on consumer protection while others, such as the Truth-In-Lending Act ("TILA") governed the disclosure of certain terms and conditions. The Fair Credit Reporting Act ("FCRA"), Equal Credit Opportunity Act ("ECOA"), Gramm Leach Bliley ("GLB") Privacy Act, and Fair Debt Collection Practices Act ("FDCPA") were just a few of the major laws that existed at the federal level. At the state level there were motor vehicle sales finance laws that governed everything from how much interest could be charged, whether additional fees such as late and returned check charges could be applied, and what other types of products could be financed. Of course, Article 9 of the Uniform Commercial Code governed the recovery of the collateral which secured these contracts.

These federal laws were primarily enforced by the Federal Trade Commission while prudential regulators such as the Texas Office of Consumer Credit Commissioner ("TX OCCC") enforced the laws of the various states. Though the industry had what I would call a healthy respect for the FTC, it didn't live in fear of it simply because the FTC didn't have the resources to devote to numerous investigations across the broad industry spectrum. From the industry's perspective, the FTC would single out a few bad actors every year and make an example of them in an effort to establish what behavior was not acceptable.

At the state level, there was a significant gap in not only the consumer protection offered but also by the level of investigations and audits conducted by the regulators. When I first became General Counsel to a national auto finance company, my frame of reference was the TX OCCC, which conducted thorough audits that involved mathematical calculations, reviews of retail installment contracts and paperwork, and even collection notes. This differed greatly from many other states, whose audits only seemed to be interested in the size of the portfolio being held so that fees and taxes could be calculated. Even when states began to see the revenue potential in these audits (somewhere around the early 2000's) it took years before they were adequately staffed to be of major concern.

Companies still got fined. They still had to be aware of the types of conduct the FTC found objectionable and be sensitive to the "hot button" issues of the various states. I won't go so far as to say that operating within that regulatory climate was a "walk in the park", but I do believe that when industry lawyers and compliance professionals look bad to life pre-CFPB, those are "the good old days".

III. Meet the New Boss.

The CFPB is certainly the most robust regulator ever faced by the auto finance industry. There are several reasons for this: first, it isn't accountable to budgetary oversight in the same way as other federal agencies because it is not funded by Congress, instead getting its funding from the Board of Governors of the Federal Reserve, pursuant to the Dodd-Frank Act. Therefore, it has grown quickly and aggressively. Secondly, its pay range is at the top of the federal pay scale, so it has been able to add more experienced personnel moving from other agencies.

The following data from its year end fiscal reports illustrates its growth: at the end of its Fiscal Year in September of 2011, it had 663 employees and received $ 161.8 Million in federal funds. By the end of its fiscal year in 2014, those numbers grew to 1,444 employees and $ 534 Million in funding. Currently, about 45% of its employees are within its Supervision, Enforcement, and Fair Lending Division. Finally, it collected $ 49.5 Million in penalties in 2013, which grew to $ 77.5 Million in FY 2014.

The industry has been irked by the examination process itself, the sheer expense of going through an examination, the fine amounts assessed to date, and the fact that Director Cordray has seemingly unlimited powers because he serves as final decision maker on whether an examination results in an enforcement action.

The process starts with the receipt of a Civil Investigative Demand ("CID"), which is like civil litigation discovery on steroids and can ask for testimony, documents, and answers to written questions. It is important to note that no evidence of wrongdoing is necessary before sending a CID. The industry is uncomfortable with the lack of opportunity to object to and limit the scope of the CID, and much like the appeals process, the Bureau is the ultimate decision maker of what is and isn't off limits. Further, while a CID isn't made public, a petition to modify or set aside a CID will be made public so a business faces quite a quandary if it wants to pursue modification.

After receiving the CID, a "meet and confer" is held within ten days. The purpose of this meeting is to go over what is expected of the business and facilitate the exam process. The industry is not comfortable with this short time frame and finds it inadequate to hire legal counsel, identify the issues, consult with management and others necessary in the process, and develop an adequate response. Much of the information needed involves computer data and the services of not only internal IT departments, but often outside resources. Again, this illustrates the burden placed on the industry, and there doesn't even have to be proof or even a claim of improper conduct.

It is at this point that the business and its representatives can seek to limit the CID and frame the scope of the inquiries. From here, the examination usually begins within sixty days, which the industry doesn't view as sufficient to adequately prepare for the level of scrutiny under which the examinee is placed.

As for the examination itself, depending on the size of the institution, a dozen or more examiners can descend upon the business. They essentially have access to the business and the ability to interview not only management but also the employees responsible for day to day operations. The examiners can investigate policies and procedures, business practices from cradle to grave, and just about anything else they want to look at.

A. The Penalties against Auto Finance Companies.

The penalties and remediation that have been levied on the industry have been staggering. While not a complete list, they include:

Drive Time	$ 8 Million
First Investors	$ 2.75 Million
Dealer Financial Svs	$ 3.3 Million
Santander	$ 9.35 Million

The range of behavior that was found punishable is a good illustration of the far reaching analysis done by the Bureau. DriveTime was the first action it took against a buy here –pay here dealer, of which DriveTime is one of the largest if not the largest, with hundreds of lots. The acts complained of involved both collections practices (harassing borrowers at work, harassing references, making excessive calls) and credit reporting (providing inaccurate information, failing to properly handle disputes, and failing to have reasonable procedures to ensure accuracy of consumer credit information). The Consent Order went so far as to examine the number of consumer credit reporting disputes the company received annually and make a comparison to the number of employees responsible for answering them and determined that staffing was not adequate for meaningful analysis to be conducted. Similarly, First Investors involved allegations of numerous credit reporting errors that the company claimed occurred as a result of computer errors with a third party vendor. Acts complained of included payments being under-stated and past due amounts being overstated, delinquency being reported as more recent than should have been, and delinquency amount and frequency both being inflated.

The Bureau has also made it clear that it will treat wrongful conduct against military members quite harshly. Dealer Financial

Services, which deals with service-members, was targeted for alleged under-stating of the cost of insurance and cost and coverage of service contracts. Similarly, Security National Automotive Acceptance Company has recently been sued by the CFPB for alleged violation of debt collection laws against service-members. Most significantly, Santander was also pursued for its handling of service-member accounts, this time related to repossession. It is notable that the significant fine and remediation imposed in that case ($ 9 million) was directly related to "only" about 1,100 accounts.

B. Disparate Impact.

Soon to be coming down the turnpike are cases against the captive finance arms of Honda, Toyota, Nissan and possibly others. (As of the deadline to send this article for publication, a $ 24 Million Dollar resolution with Honda has been announced, with Honda agreeing to limit dealer mark-ups going forward). Based on information already released, it looks as if companies like this and other third party finance companies will have to limit how much they allow dealers to increase the cost of auto financing. The CFPB alleges that there is unintentional discrimination against minority consumers based on a theory known as disparate impact. The practice refers to allowing dealers to set their own amount of dealer reserve – the share of a buyer's interest rate that the dealer earns for arranging the financing, which may result in some minority groups paying higher interest rates. The CFPB views this practice as discriminatory if it has an adverse effect on minority groups, even if unintentional.

Some banks and other companies have already announced that they will do away with dealer mark-ups and move to flat rates so that there is no potential for any consumer paying a higher rate.

C. Vendors and other Third Parties.

The CFPB has also put the industry on notice that the supervised entities are going to be responsible for the actions of their vendors and other third party service providers. The First Investors matter made it very clear that they won't accept an attempt to lay the blame on the software or any other vendor. The Bureau has published guidelines for managing these third party relationships and its examinations guidelines share how they will drill down to this level. This is especially meaningful in an industry where many of the services that impact consumers the most, like repossessions and credit reporting, are outsourced to third parties.

As a result, the industry participants have had to re-examine their practices and those of their vendors. The level of scrutiny and due diligence have increased greatly. For instance, where as before, it would have been common practice to look at a repossession companies list of clients and success rate before hiring them, now creditors should pay closer attention to the vendors policies, how they go about hiring employees, their Better Business Bureau or other ratings, and history of litigation and resolution. This has added substantial cost to the bottom line and also added a new layer of complexity to the ability of these companies to do business.

D. Consumer Complaints.

The CFPB has taken a great interest in the subject of consumer complaints and has made a significant investment by adding features to its website that will accept complaints from consumers and make the actions of creditors transparent to the public. Its consumer complaint database allows consumers to provide a narrative on their dispute, including the name of the company involved and specific bad acts of which they complain. Further, the CFPB has encouraged finance companies to participate in this process by registering on the site and participating in the resolution process.

The industry has expressed concern over the CFPB's methods because it believes the narrative complaints are unsupported and one sided. It's been argued that these complaints are analogous to what used to be submitted to the Better Business Bureau or online complaint repositories, except that by appearing on the CFPB website they are given an air of legitimacy, while, in fact, they are unsubstantiated and one-sided. Additionally, some in the industry feel trapped, in essence, because an adequate response to a complaint may necessitate sharing details regarding the account which are private and can't be shared publicly. Finally, critics argue that the numbers being reported by the Bureau are skewed, with the largest institutions naturally receiving the largest number of complaints.

The Bureau has also directed companies to develop and implement a complaint management system to track complaints and demonstrate resolution. More critically, it has been made clear that this system will be the subject of CID's and audited so that companies are accountable for their responsiveness to complaints. It isn't too far-fetched to think that, much like the credit dispute handling issue in DriveTime, companies will be judged on whether they have adequately staffed this function.

E. Compliance Management Systems.

Much like Sarbanes-Oxley has been credited with creating a cottage industry for corporate accountants and leading to rampant cost increases, the CFPB's mandate of the need for entities to develop a Compliance Management System ("CMS") has already made quite an impact. Everyone from small independent buy here –pay here car dealers to large financial institutions are trying to figure out what this means to their business. An army of lawyers and compliance experts have descended on the industry like locusts on a field.

The CFPB requires these companies to have a program "designed to ensure that the financial institutions policies and practices are in full compliance with the requirements of Federal consumer financial law". A robust CMS would establish compliance responsibilities, communicate them to the employees, and work the legal requirements for the business into its operational practices. This is a significant undertaking because of the numerous Federal laws that touch upon auto finance, such as TILA, ECOA, FCRA, OFAC and GLB, just to name a few.

When properly created, the CMS would demonstrate how a dealership:

- Establishes compliance responsibilities;
- Communicates them to employees;

- Ensures that responsibilities for meeting legal requirements and internal policies are incorporated into business processes;
- Reviews operations to ensure that legal requirements are met; and
- Takes corrective action and updates systems as necessary.

The CFPB has set out four control components it wishes to see:

- Ownership/board and management oversight;
- Compliance programs conducted;
- Consumer Complaint tracking and response;
- Compliance audits, policy reviews, corrective action, and policy and procedure modifications, when appropriate.

The CFPB has recognized that this isn't a "one size fits all" approach, and that the complexity of the CMS can be tailored to fit the size and lines of business served. The Bureau has made clear, though, that not only does it expect to see a qualified compliance officer guiding these efforts, but that these efforts should be driven from the top to bottom of the company, so that every employee is part of the compliance efforts. Further, it wants the compliance officer to have direct access to senior management. Again, much like the point it made in DriveTime, companies will need to be able to demonstrate that it has adequately staffed compliance resources sufficient for the size and scope of its operations.

The impact of this initiative has been felt from the largest financial institutions to the smaller operations, as companies have had to build an infrastructure for:

- Creation and adoption of policies and procedure manuals;
- Identifying applicable laws and analyzing compliance;
- Appointing or hiring of adequately trained personnel;
- Development of training initiatives;
- Gathering, tracking, analysis and resolution of consumer complaints;
- Management and oversight of vendors that perform functions;
- Development of reporting metrics;
- Senior management/board oversight.

For larger companies that had much of this content already in place, one of the biggest challenges was coordinating all of the information in a format that can be demonstrated, if necessary. Significant investment had to be made in training and the learning of new roles. Outside relationships, such as those with collection and repossession agencies, had to be studied to make sure that the policies and procedures of those providers matched up with the emphasis on compliance. The smaller operations, in some cases, had to start from the ground up by creating the policies and procedures, identifying who would be responsible and accountable for the compliance function, and developing a process for communicating the message throughout its organization. Employees shouldn't simply be "deputized" as compliance specialists, they need to be given adequate training and supervision so that they learn to perform their jobs.

This can perhaps all be best summed up by sharing that while attending a lobbying function sponsored by the National Independent Auto Dealers Association, an interaction took place between a Congressman and a small car dealer. The Congressman asked the car dealer "how's business", and the dealer responded "I couldn't tell you, I'm too busy focusing on compliance".

IV. How Far is the Reach?

It is not an overstatement to say that every dealership or finance company will be affected by the CFPB. Some may plan on conducting business as usual and don't think they'll ever have any direct dealings with the CFPB. Their logic is that the CFPB will never show up in "name that town, USA" and that they'll never receive a CID or be subjected to any type of direct oversight. While all of that may very well be true, it is still foolish of any entity involved in car finance to think that it will remain untouched.

First, companies don't simply work in a vacuum. Maybe a dealer sells its paper every so often. If it does, you can bet that the purchaser will conduct due diligence and want to see the seller's CMS and other content to demonstrate it follows the relevant laws.

Many dealers do business with vendors like GPS/starter interrupt devices or other type products. Those companies are concerned that they are subject to supervision of the Bureau because of the products and services they offer and have begun to ramp up due diligence on their own relationships. I worked for a technology company that provided a dealer management system ("DMS"), which is essentially the hub of the dealer's business, and we were very concerned with the scrutiny we and our clients would be subject to and made changes to our business to be able to demonstrate our commitment to compliance.

It's pretty routine for dealer's to pull credit reports, report on consumer performance, or do both, so those businesses are all subject to the changing world of credit reporting that was brought about by the Bureau's initial efforts to hold the credit reporting agencies accountable for the content of those reports and the increased standards that the agencies have developed as a result.

Secondly, the Bureau has working arrangements with numerous state and local regulators across the country and have information sharing agreements. This means that information about financing products and services is passed back and forth for further action. While the CFPB may not show up in "name that town, USA, you can bet it would take an interest if that specific regulator uncovered abusive business practices and called it to the attention of the Bureau. The past few years has brought a significant increase in the depth of audits conducted on these businesses. Further, these regulators are now not just focused on simple things like usury and late fees, but are asking for more detailed information about things like adverse action, add-on products, and disposition of collateral after repossession. Investigation of this depth happens regularly so the impact is much more widespread than just those unlucky enough to find themselves within the Bureau's cross-hairs.

The CFPB's investment in its consumer complaint database makes scrutiny even more likely, as it publishes lists like its top ten complaint types and businesses named in complaints on a monthly basis. Data it shares is then picked up by local and national news, as well as organizations like the National Consumer Law Center, so that even a one-sided consumer narrative can be considered newsworthy if it's juicy enough.

Perhaps most important, the vast majority of them rely on banks and other sources of capital to run their business. These institutions come in a wide range of sizes, from large national banks to smaller community banks to private equity firms. All of those firms care a lot about what the CFPB says and how it thinks, either because they are supervised entities or because they are subject to oversight from another government regulator.

I can tell you firsthand that the past few years have seen a tremendous change on how the capital providers do business. A lot more emphasis is being placed on due diligence and meaningful questions are being asked of those that originate and hold the paper. For instance, I've taken calls from dealers undergoing audits that are being asked how their DMS was programmed to handle certain situations and to provide proof of various calculations. We also had to provide written responses to questions about our data security and process work flow charts. This is all much more in depth than anything we'd experience previously.

Remember, these sources of capital are big businesses that manage their risk, so they've added compliance and legal staff to help ferret out those whose business operations aren't aligned with these compliance values. If the dealer's want their money, and want to get it at a more favorable rate, they are going to have to demonstrate their commitment to compliance, even if they never end up as a direct target of the Bureau.

V. What's the Industry to Do?

In my opinion, the most important thing these companies can do is to recognize that their business climate has changed and accept the fact that they can't ignore what is going on around them. Those that turn a blind eye are taking a significant risk. A pro-active approach doesn't have to be prohibitively expensive but it is going to require the investment of not only financial resources but also the attention of management.

The CFPB has published examination guidelines to help regulated entities prepare for the process. These are a valuable tool for any company, not just those that are in danger of a direct audit. By studying these guidelines one can learn the "hot button" issues and conduct an internal examination. Also, a lot can be learned by simply studying the published consent orders. They give a clear indication of what issues are on the Bureau's radar and the depth to which attention is being paid to particular business practices.

While certainly not a comprehensive list, it's reasonable to say that the following are some best practices that should be adopted:

- Appoint a Compliance Officer and provide adequate training in the form of materials and outside training or classes;
- Give the Compliance Officer authority equal to other senior managers;
- Develop regular communication between compliance officer and management;
- Track changes to process made as a result of industry developments;
- Identify and audit key points of business based on Bureau written guidance and actions;
- Review of all policy and procedure manuals;

- Review job descriptions;
- Develop training for all departments, paying special attention to those that have customer interaction;
- Creation of a Compliance Management System that supports culture of compliance;
- Utilize progressive discipline for violations of compliance policies and procedures;
- Develop and coordinate a Complaint Management System so that all employees know what constitutes a compliant, how to record one and how to resolve one;
- Look for commonality within customer complaints;
- Illustrate when consumer complaints are used for process improvement;
- Learn how to conduct due diligence on any outside vendors, review their contracts, and conduct outside audits;
- Terminate outside vendors whose compliance values don't match;
- Evaluate customer service and ease of customers communicating with business;
- Coordinate with outside professionals;
- Join industry groups and subscribe to industry publications.

By adopting these measures, companies will be in a much better position when scrutiny comes from capital providers, regulators or anyone else in a position to investigate because they will be able to demonstrate that a culture of compliance exists and it is the intention of the business to conduct itself with the consumer's interests in mind.

VI. What Does this Mean for the Plaintiff's Bar?

There is unprecedented transparency into the business practices of car dealers and auto finance companies. A regulator with a big stick that isn't afraid to use it has loosened a lot of teeth. This regulator's interests are aligned with the Plaintiff's bar. After all, both the Bureau and Plaintiff's lawyers are in the business of protecting consumers.

As a result, these businesses are gathering more information about themselves and their practices. The Bureau has essentially published a best practices manual for the industry, in the form of its examination guidelines, and fairly regularly publishes written guidance in the form of consent orders and litigation. This serves as a treasure trove for the Plaintiff's bar.

A Plaintiff's lawyer pursuing a case against one of these businesses would be wise to study this material and use it as a starting point for litigation strategy. While a small buy here – pay here dealer isn't expected to possess the same sophistication as a larger company, it should have sufficient policies and procedures, training of personnel, supervision of its vendors, and awareness of the current "hot topic" issues going on in the industry. All of those items are fair game in discovery and have been for years.

The difference is that now there is seemingly a cohesive voice advocating consumer protection and taking action against those it feels haven't measured up. This is quite a contrast to the former myriad of Federal and state regulators with various degrees of interest. The wise Plaintiff's lawyer will tap into the pulse and look at these cases in the larger context of how the industry is evolving in the area of compliance and best practices rather than pursue these claims on a "one off" basis with no regard for how the paradigm has shifted.

LET'S CREATE A NATIONAL LENDER'S DAY!

On a recent Sunday, while watching a football game, I learned during a commercial break that November 3rd had been chosen as National Sandwich Day. By whom? Is there an organization that makes these decisions? Was it made up by the national sandwich chain mentioned in the commercials? Can we blame Hallmark for this?

The commercial got me thinking, though, and I've decided that the consumer finance industry should create a National Lender's Day as a way to combat the bad press, misinformation, and regulatory attacks that we as an industry endure. As a counter-attack, we should join together and create a day that acknowledges the essential role lenders play in our economy. In my mind, there are three essential aspects to our celebratory day.

Lender's Play an Important Role

First, we need to call attention to the critical contribution we make in the lives of all consumers and the impact our financial products and services have on both the lives of consumers and the ability of this country to do business. After all, it is our industry that allows people to go to work, kids to get to school and so forth. How should we accomplish the monumental task of favorable media coverage in the face of largely media generated public perception that lenders are irresponsible, predatory, and just plain mean? In my humble opinion, all consumer Lenders need to cease all underwriting and extensions of credit for the day. That means no making of loans, no buying of paper, and no underwriting. Take the day off, budgets be damned!

Why? Because maybe then the public, press and regulators will appreciate the service that the industry provides instead of constantly attacking it. Maybe then they'll wake up and realize that there is such a thing as personal accountability and that in the real world many people do take their financial commitments seriously. Instead, we've been placed in a no-win situation where just about every loan/contract or other credit instrument is a ticking time bomb from a regulatory perspective. Was underwriting done correctly? Was there discriminatory intent or effect? Can the consumer afford to pay back this loan? Are lenders going too far in trying to collect these obligations? These "Monday morning Quarterbacking" questions are now part of our norm. So let's take a "pass" for the day. One less day of originations is one less day of risk!

If Regulators, legislators, the press or consumers have a problem with this, it's simple enough to explain that by instituting this holiday we are trying to provide a public service and prevent soon to be "bad" loans from being made. Granted, this holiday from extending credit will be a hardship for the public because they rely on our industry to help make ends meet on a daily basis, but if they want to protest they can write their Congressman, picket the CFPB, or even post a complaint on its website. After all, there is no constitutional right to receive credit.

A Day of Learning Instead of Lending

The second key aspect of this special day is for the industry to illustrate its commitment to compliance and following the telephone book sized bevy of applicable rules by making this a day of learning. Sorry, no visits to the beach or favorite pub. Everybody involved in originations must spend the day reading recent consent decrees and CFPB proposed rules and examination guidelines. This may sound expensive to lenders, but the costs of compliance have already multiplied exponentially, this just allows companies to focus on it for one day instead of trying to run a business while at the same time keeping up with the governmental mandates. Even better, how can the press attack the industry's attempt at self-improvement? We can even create standardized testing and publish test scores to illustrate our commitment to do our jobs better.

The Power of Positive Press

Thirdly, we need to have an all-out media blitz sharing our side of the story. We can out-sensationalize the New York Times. We'll share anecdotal stories of some of the people we help! We can shine the light on the family that can't make ends meet without small bridge loans or the single parent that was able to get a better job because affordable transportation was provided by a buy-here pay-here car dealer, or maybe the executive that got their start because they were able to procure an education loan. We can even focus on the importance of personal accountability and how it is up to each individual to accurately assess their financial situation and ability to repay because, after-all, they know the true facts of their life better than any underwriter.

How Would the CFPB React?

I fear, though, that our special day would be short-lived. Surely the CFPB would step in and ban the holiday because of the harm it would do to consumers. After-all, if consumer's can't procure financing, then they can't consume, which would give the CFPB less folks to protect, and there's got to be something in Dodd-Frank that prohibits that result.

Admittedly, some of this is tongue and cheek, but I am intrigued by the concept. As an industry we've got to do something other than accept the cards we've been dealt. What do the lenders say? Is anyone willing to forgo a day of originations to make a point?

HOW FAR IS TOO FAR?

The CFPB has taken things too far. No, I'm not talking about its recent announcement looking to do away with class action waivers in arbitration clauses. I'm not talking about the $ 40 Million Dollars plus in refunds and fines in the recent Westlake/ Wilshire consent decree. I'm not even talking about the zeal with which they are pursuing disparate impact cases despite the fact that the basis of their claims rests on questionable analytics. No, I'm talking about something much more basic yet crucial to our system of justice, namely, the attorney-client relationship and access to courts.

Although it hasn't gathered the headlines that the multi-million dollar penalties do, the CFPB has chosen to pursue several law firms that provide legal services to creditors, debt buyers and debt collectors. These law firms file lots of lawsuits against consumers on behalf of some very large clients. By choosing to pursue these law firms the Bureau is attempting to insert itself right in the middle of the attorney-client relationship. The CFPB seems to be saying that the attorneys' representing these companies should know that practices like "robo-signing" (having personnel sign lots of affidavits without adequate investigation), are taking place. Even more dangerous, it is alleging that the lawyers representing these companies have little or no meaningful involvement in these cases based on the sheer number of cases they file.

This is a slippery slope and inserts the CFPB into regulation of attorneys, which should be left to the American Bar Association and State Bar Associations that license lawyers. That's right, lawyers are licensed by the various states, and are obligated to follow a litany of rules, many of which involve attorney ethics and the attorney-client relationship. If lawyers violate the rules they are obligated to follow, they are subject to discipline by those that have been given the power by the government to regulate them, namely the various Bar Associations.

The CFPB, though, is attempting to bring lawyers within its realm based on the fact that they represent creditors and others whose interests are in conflict with consumers. This feels strikingly similar to its efforts to regulate franchise car dealers because their products are financed, even though franchise car dealers were carved out of Dodd Frank, which is from where the Bureau itself was created. The consumer finance industry needs to understand this is taking place and appreciate the danger it represents.

Although the Bureau's marching orders are to protect consumers, it is a concern when it seeks to infringe on the lawful rights of those whose interests are adverse to consumers. Creditors and consumers naturally have adverse interests when consumers fail to make payments or honor other obligations. These companies have a right to pursue legal remedies in court, when necessary. These companies should be free to hire lawyers and law firms of their own choosing. The actions of the CFPB will, if allowed to continue, inhibit the ability of these companies to do so and will increase the costs of obtaining representation of their choosing.

Before becoming an in-house compliance lawyer, I spent the first ten years of my career in private practice representing car dealers, banks, and finance companies. I filed lots of lawsuits against consumers for non-payment of accounts, judicial recovery of vehicles, protecting interests in bankruptcy court, and other actions. My job involved preparation of the pleadings setting forth the case, which often needed to be supported by an affidavit of a representative of the client that had personal knowledge of the account.

I'd provide the form of the affidavit, because I was familiar with the rules of court and knew what needed to be included for a judge to find it sufficient. My job wasn't to examine the policies and procedures of the company and determine whether they were adequate or if the person signing the affidavit followed them. Nor was I aware of how many other affidavits the representative signed that day, or how many other lawsuits the company filed that day, whether they be filed throughout the country, my state, or even in my county. Yet that seems to be the standard the CFPB is seeking to impose on lawyers representing creditors. Put simply, it is trying to force litigation lawyers to become experts in the compliance standards of their clients.

In litigation, issues like what steps the company representative took to investigate the account and how much time was spent on the investigation are appropriate for discovery, which is the stage where the parties look to pick apart the other side's case. The CFPB, under the guise of consumer "protection", seems to want to change the rules of our system, though, and safeguard consumers from the companies through regulation of their attorneys', which naturally have interests that are adverse to the consumer.

Some that side with the CFPB like to point out that attorneys collecting debts are already regulated by the Fair Debt Collection Practices Act; however, there is a significant distinction between lawyers choosing to undertake efforts to collect a debt directly from a consumer outside of court and lawyers that utilize the court system to do so. This distinction needs to be preserved.

If it isn't, where would things end? Would companies and their law firms be subject to penalties for filing "too many" lawsuits? Would the CFPB look to punish companies as well as law firms that have a strong track record of obtaining Reaffirmation Agreements from debtors in Chapter 7 bankruptcies or for filing Motions to Lift Stay in bankruptcy cases? After all, these methods are "harassing" in the eyes of a Bureau whose sole mandate is to defend the consumer! Would companies still be able to pursue lawful garnishments to collect deficient accounts? Would companies that aggressively utilize judicial repossession be disciplined for seeking judicial intervention when it is the actions of the consumer that has prevented collateral recovery? Would the CFPB argue it has supervisory authority over lawyers representing these companies? Would companies still be able to retain the law firms of their choosing, or would the CFPB look unfavorably upon using certain law firms that have a track record not to its liking? Would there be any law firms left willing to represent creditors, and if so, at what price? Like I said, it's a slippery slope.

Finally, a word of caution to the plaintiff's bar before it gets too enthusiastically behind this CFPB initiative: ask yourselves whether the slippery slope leads right to your doorway. When money is involved the interests of the plaintiff's bar and their consumer clients diverge. What's to stop the Bureau from limiting contingency fees in consumer cases because the consumers deserve more of the settlements and awards? Or limiting the hourly amount that can be billed? Or establishing a ratio that ties attorneys' fees to the amount in controversy? Once the pandora's box is open it's difficult to limit the effects.

CFPB ACTION AGAINST LAW FIRMS WILL IMPACT YOUR BUSINESS!

In the November/December 2015 issue of this publication, I challenged the CFPB's pursuit of enforcement actions against law firms that represent creditors in debt collection suits and asked the question "How Far is Too Far"? That article pointed out the dangers the CFPB's approach presented to the judicial system, the importance of the preservation of the attorney-client relationship and the ability of creditors' to freely retain counsel. These actions have now resulted in the CFPB entering into separate consent orders with law firms Pressler & Pressler and Frederick J Hanna and Associates, P.C. that included significant monetary fines ($ 1,000,000. against Pressler & Pressler and $ 3,100,000. against Hanna) and rules they must follow when bringing future litigation against consumers. Although the orders are only applicable to these firms, I believe they contain guidance that will fundamentally change the attorney-client relationship and how creditors pursue litigation against consumers in default.

Background.

By way of background, both of these law firms are debt collections law firms that collect debt on behalf of creditors such as banks, credit card issuers, and companies that purchase and sell consumer debt, and they filed hundreds of thousands of lawsuits in just the past several years. The Bureau characterized Pressler & Pressler as "churning out unfair and deceptive debt collection lawsuits based on flimsy or non-existent evidence". Similarly, the CFPB's Press Release referred to Hanna as "a lawsuit mill" and stated "Debt collectors that use the court system for purposes of intimidation should reconsider how their practices are harming consumers". Obviously, the Bureau doesn't like their robust business model.

The CFPB's Allegations.

The CFPB attacked the law firms for a litany of alleged deceptive and abusive conduct when bringing cases against consumers, including:

- mass producing lawsuits with automated systems used by non-attorney support staff with little meaningful attorney involvement;
- called attention to the fact that in some cases the attorney reviewed the file for less than 30 seconds before initiating a lawsuit (Pressler);
- One attorney signed over 130,000 debt collection lawsuits over a two year period (Hanna);
- filing lawsuits without a sufficient basis and without review of underlying documents;
- filing lawsuits on unreliable or false information; and
- filing lawsuits based on affidavits that in some cases the signers couldn't have known the facts they were attesting to.

Practices the Firms Must Now Follow.

The final orders in both cases, which are very similar, go into great detail describe the level of detail these firms must follow when bringing debt collection litigation going forward, including:

- they must possess specific account level documentation;
- they must possess the contractual terms and conditions applicable to the debt if pursuing a breach of contract claim;
- they must possess what essentially amounts to a "chain of title" with corresponding bills of sale and chronological listing when pursuing collection suits on behalf of debt buyers;
- confirmation that the consumer's debt has not been discharged in bankruptcy or is pending to a pending bankruptcy proceeding;
- use of methods or means to accurately determine the consumer's correct identity and address to determine appropriate venue;
- attorney confirmation that the statute of limitations has not expired in the case;
- the signing attorney's use of software that would create an electronic record noting that the initiation of the collection suit complies with the Order;
- several conditions relating to affidavits used in collection cases to ensure that the affiants have personal knowledge of the facts attested to, the review of account level

documentation, and execution of the affidavit in the presence of a notary;

- training of all employees and outside counsel for compliance with the Order; and
- the Hanna order sets forth a requirement that an annual review of the process and procedures of any entity that employs affiants executing and submitting affidavits for use in collection suits initiated by the firm to ensure compliance with the provisions of the Order related to affidavits.

General Applicability.

Director Cordray has previously stated that consent orders are detailed guidance for the industry and that those who do not heed their warnings are committing "compliance malpractice". Therefore, these decrees need to be looked at in terms of the broader war that the Bureau is fighting on behalf of consumers against the collection industry. It would be a mistake to think that they have limited applicability because they involve different types of financial products and aged debt.

It is apparent that the CFPB rejects the technology and other efficiencies used by these law firms to file mass numbers of cases. Many of the requirements placed on these law firms require less use of non-lawyer staff and systems and more meaningful attorney involvement in the cases prior to filing, which will slow down the number of cases being filed and, in all probability, change the economics for both law firms and their clients. As it has done previously in other matters, the CFPB has changed the business paradigm without having to issue a single rule, and it's up to the industry participants to figure out what change is needed in its business.

Recommendations.

Litigation against consumers is often a last resort and may even be the only way to recover a car or to get a consumer to honor a contract. Whether it's judicial foreclosure of a vehicle or pursuit of the underlying debt, though, finance companies need to build some protections into their practices that take into account what the CFPB has set forth in these Orders.

Regular readers of this publication already know about the CFPB's expectations for companies that use outside vendors. Treat law firms like other outside vendors and conduct due diligence. Ask them about their staffing, level of attorney involvement, volume of litigation, processes and procedures, and steps they've taken as a result of these cases. It may be necessary to re-write representation agreements to mandate attorney involvement and include service level agreements. Likewise, finance companies and other creditors should expect that their vendor law firms are going to mandate that account level information is provided upon the referral of a case and may ask the companies to warrant and represent a level of staff involvement and familiarity with each case. Both parties are going to be able to demonstrate that these issues were considered when deciding to pursue litigation against consumers.

It's critical that the creditor/plaintiff examine its internal practices surrounding document management, execution of affidavits, actual knowledge surrounding the file being referred, and even the process by which cases are selected to be referred. It's beneficial to have an objective written policy that spells out how cases are chosen and the basic documentation and other requirements to be provided to counsel. Although concepts like an affiant having personal knowledge of facts aren't new, the rules of procedure already require them, but it is probably a good idea to spell out the expectations for employees signing affidavits.

The requirement of annual review of the creditors' policies and procedures for affidavits found in the Hanna Order presents a conundrum because it seems to be giving law firms compliance responsibility over its clients and has the potential to place lawyer and client in an adversarial position. Though the requirement seems to be ripe for challenge if the CFPB attempts to hold others to such a standard, it shouldn't be ignored. It's probably a good idea for the parties to build this into the representation agreement and demonstrate good intent.

Finally, those of you that buy or sell contracts or debt, or may wish to do so in the future, will need to carefully study these cases. It will be a requirement to be able to produce a chronological chain of title from inception forward. Careful consideration of the seller's previous document practices will be needed. Additionally, beware of the potential risk presented by sale/purchase of the paper and the danger of counter-claims and violation of representations and warranties found in the transaction documents.

Conclusion.

Now is the time for companies to be proactive and take a critical look at their document management systems, policies and procedures over both choosing cases to forward to counsel for litigation as well as how such law firms are chosen, and develop best practices for creating and signing affidavits to be used in debt collection litigation. Law firms and clients are going to have to collaborate to make sure that procedures are in place that are consistent with the vision set forth by the CFPB. At least for the time being, the fight is over and it's best for business to adapt and strengthen these practices.

WHERE DO WE GO FROM HERE?

A Look at Consumer Protection in the Trump Administration

By now we've all seen the news footage of thousands of consumer Plaintiff's lawyers marching on the Capitol to protest President Trump's announcement that the CFPB will be downsized, as well as the resulting tragically sad pictures of the hundreds of CFPB employees walking out of its Washington D.C. headquarters with boxes carrying their personal belongings. Oh, wait, that hasn't happened, but I bet I got your attention.

I wrote this tongue in cheek introduction as a result of conversations I've had with many industry folks that seem to think that we've "won" the war, the CFPB will be emasculated and business can get "back to normal". Sorry to disagree, but while I think there will soon be some critical changes, the CFPB will continue to be alive and kicking. Why? For one thing, government agencies just usually don't go away. They may get re-named and re-tasked maybe, but not simply tossed aside. That means there are still well over 1,000 CFPB employees that are in the business of consumer protection and take their jobs seriously.

It would be wise to remember that the Bureau still has some pretty strong and powerful supporters within the government that will fight on its behalf, including its creator, Senator Warren, who is thought to be a Democratic front runner in four years and seemingly takes every available opportunity to pontificate on the virtues of the Bureau and the evils of the consumer finance industry. Since the Bureau, in my view, is not going to simply disappear, let's start the New Year by taking a look at how things might progress under the new administration and what it means for the auto finance industry. These are just my opinions and views and from the time I write this to the time it gets published there may be events that transpire that prove me wrong. That's the chance I take by writing for a print publication.

I do think that Director Cordray will be leaving the Bureau in the near term. He may choose to leave to pursue a run for Governor of Ohio, or President Trump may pro-actively remove him, but either way he will not remain Director. I also believe that there will be a movement within Congress to reshape the Bureau in many ways, among them to replace the Director position with a bi-partisan panel of Commissioners, similar to other government agencies like the Federal Trade Commission (FTC). This change alone will have a significant impact because prior to joining the CFPB, Director Cordray already had a career long strong background in consumer advocacy and protection from his days as Attorney General of Ohio and, as the sole Director, he had unilateral power to set policy and act at judge, jury and executioner. The fact that President Trump and a Republican controlled Congress would play a significant role in naming the Commissioners leads me to believe that the next leaders will not share Director Cordray's background or industry-view.

As a result, and in combination with expected Congressional action to bring the Bureau's budget under control and make it more accountable to Congress, I think that there will be a movement to curtail some of the Bureau's more robust and aggressive practices such as using Consent Decrees to make "laws" instead of going through the more stringent rulemaking process. I also expect that there will be some retreat from Director Cordray's statement that ignoring Consent Decrees is "compliance malpractice". Hopefully, this will result in a more fair and balanced approach from the Bureau and take business practicalities into consideration while protecting consumers. For instance, small finance companies simply don't have the resources available to meet some of the expectations set forth in Consent Decrees between the CFPB and some of the industry's biggest members.

I also expect to see a retreat from the Bureau's position on fair lending in the auto space and its reliance on both geo-coding and flawed mathematics to support its own conclusions. While Fair Lending will continue to get a lot of attention, I suspect that new leaders would look for better data and not be so quick to "find" disparate impact. While I'm not sure whether this will curb the move towards flat fees and away from discounts, I do hope there will be more of an emphasis on fairness instead of using consumer "protection" as a hammer.

Similarly, I expect to see a softening of the Bureau's position on arbitration to be more accepting of their use. The Bureau has spent a significant amount of resources on its report, so the issue won't be dropped, but I anticipate that new leadership will be more receptive of the arguments set forth by the industry, and will also be more willing to consider the effect of some larger thematic type issues such as the cost and time of litigation and the recovery by consumers using alternative dispute resolution as compared to class action members. So don't scrap those arbitration clauses in your retail installment contracts just yet, there is a lot of game left to be played.

Likewise, I expect to see more consideration of industry viewpoints in the area of third party collections. The 1,000 plus pages of materials published by the CFPB a few months ago was daunting and would have necessitated a paradigm shift. While I do expect that a majority of the proposed protections will remain, I do think new leadership will give more consideration to practical issues and the costs to the industry. Simply put, I think the initiative to revamp third party collections will continue but the final result will not be as draconian as first proposed. I also think that rules related to first party collections will be delayed and are not as imminent as we thought just a few months ago.

I do believe that the CFPB's zealous concern for complaint management will continue. Some practices might change, such as what information is available on the complaint database and its use, but the subject of complaint management will remain critical and, quite frankly, that's a good thing. After having helped many companies of various sizes and complexities establish or fine tune their complaint management policies and implementing them, I am of the firm belief that this is just practicing good business and is good for business. Not only does strong complaint management cut down lawsuits and, therefore, risk, it leads to increased customer satisfaction. Sorry to be a contrarian thinker among many of you, but I do think this is an area where the Bureau's attention has been well spent and has made a beneficial difference for both the industry and consumers.

My feelings are pretty similar on the subject of vendor management. Here again, the CFPB gets credit for shining a light on an issue that needed attention. Up until the last few years, there was a lot of inherent risk in the way many industry members used third party service providers and the industry, as a whole, didn't do a good job in identifying those risks. The CFPB has sought to change this, and those that have been proactive are better for it (well, maybe not some vendors) and I think the emphasis will continue. For those of you wanting to cast aspersions in my direction for my point of view, I suggest it would be a better use of your time to develop a strong vendor management program.

Finally, over the past few years we've been bludgeoned with the importance of industry participants having a Compliance Management System (CMS). The cornerstones of Board oversight, a compliance program, consumer complaint response, and audit have been tattooed into our consciousness, and I don't see that diminishing. While I do think that there should be some meaningful details and practical examples added to the general Bureau statement that the steps taken should be appropriate for the "size and complexity of the business", the overall emphasis will remain and, again, I look at that as a positive. These concepts are not painful and really do make for better businesses.

In summary, I do envision a Congressional movement that will make some significant changes to the way the CFPB operates that will have a big impact on how it regulates our industry going forward. At the same time, the Bureau employs well over 1,000 people and they are mostly pretty zealous advocates on behalf of the consumer, so don't expect the Bureau to put its tail between its legs for four years. Also, there are a lot of moving pieces, both politically and within the industry, so keep a close eye on developments over the next year. The content of this article are my thoughts and best guesses, and are certainly open to debate and argument.

MEET THE NEW BOSS - SAME AS THE OLD BOSS

What Can We Expect from the Biden Administration?

The Who song "Won't Get Fooled Again" ends with the words that I've chosen to be the title to this article, and through them Pete Townshend sums up the subject of revolution by seemingly saying "the more things change, the more they stay the same".

I have been thinking about these lyrics a lot lately as I contemplate the coming regulatory changes in our auto finance world. A Biden administration means that consumer advocates (dare I say zealots) will once again have the ears of those in power and in many cases be the ones in power, just like they were during the Obama Presidency. The Trump Presidency's drive to rollback regulation is over and we can expect to see more efforts to direct what's permissible (and harsh guidance on what's not) when selling and financing vehicles. I hope that those who were "fooled" into a false sense of complacency during the Trump years are ready to do the work necessary to please the New Boss.

As I write this Biden is President-Elect and we are in the middle of transition. It is highly likely that CFPB Director Kraninger will be replaced early in the Biden Administration, and we can bet that a new Director will hold principles very similar to former Director Cordray and Senator Warren, who was instrumental in the creation of the Bureau, hence my choice for the title and theme of this article. For those of you who need a history refresher, that leadership period of the CFPB was known for aggressive consumer protection through a practice that came to be referred to as "regulation by enforcement", with the Bureau deterring what it perceived as wrongful conduct across the industry with highly publicized and Draconian actions against individual companies rather than by promulgating clear rules.

That Bureau aggressively pursued theories based on disparate impact, discrimination, and ability to repay arguments. That Bureau issued severe penalties for what it found to be "abusive" conduct, even though "abusive" wasn't defined. It was gearing up for a challenge to widespread use of arbitration clauses by creditors. It published debt collection rules that blurred the lines between first and third party collections and demonstrated an intent to promulgate restrictions that would have fundamentally changed the way debts were collected. In the minds of those running things prior to the 2016 election, a Clinton Presidency was going to allow it to continue down these paths, and it had quite a robust consumer protection agenda.

My belief is that new Bureau leadership will pick up right where they left off in 2016, and we can expect more of the same. Coupled with an FTC that's been more active in the area of consumer financial protection over the past few years, state regulators that have increased their scrutiny of the lending industry, new mini-CFPB's being created at the state level, and a generation of plaintiffs' lawyers that studied the CFPB's playbook on what constitutes bad conduct by lenders, and it appears that we're going to have to navigate some treacherous waters over the next few years. Plus, the new CFPB leadership will certainly have more to say about servicing, collecting and even underwriting practices during the pandemic

So what's a BHPH dealer to do? My advice is to do your BEST, and I don't say that flippantly. Your businesses come in many different models and sizes. I don't expect a dealership with 10 employees to have the same compliance resources as one with 100 employees, but I think each one has to make its BEST effort to have a demonstrable compliance program that is appropriate for the "size and complexity of its business", as the CFPB has itself said.

When a dealership has to defend itself, whether it's a lawsuit or a regulator action, the key is to demonstrate all the steps that have been taken to attempt to get things right. That means having a written plan for compliance, policies and procedures that show there is a commitment to doing things the right way, conducting personnel training to engrain the "right way" in daily operations, doing some audits or assessments to verify that the business is operating as it should, and facilitating a company culture that believes in treating customers in a fair and transparent manner.

I challenge each of you to re-read that last paragraph and honestly ask yourself whether you are doing your best to achieve this goal. Discuss this with your leadership team, take a look at each department or business function and make a list of areas where you are strong and those in which you may be deficient. Then take steps to close those gaps. It's not enough to "know" you are doing it right, approach it as if you will have to present and prove it to a judge and jury one day, which means your plan has to be written and demonstrable.

The New Boss is going to be tough, a lot like the Boss before the last one. If we are going to thrive over these next several years, and make no mistake, the goal is to thrive, not just survive, then it's up to each of you to play a leadership role in this effort. One of the first things I tell clients is that compliance isn't something that can be bought. Sure, I can lay out the plan, but the client is the one that has to dedicate resources to get it done. 2021 is the time to meet this challenge head-on. Protect your business and make it your goal to end the year with a stronger commitment to demonstrable compliance.

2021 AND THE ROAD AHEAD

The change in Presidential administrations will result in many significant challenges in the coming years for independent vehicle dealers, so I thought I'd summarize some of the impactful initiatives that I see just over the horizon. Thematically, I will focus on the renewed emphasis on consumer protection throughout the federal and state landscape.

Consumer protection was emphasized during the Obama administration, the result being not only robust use of the CFPB to curb industry practices it deemed harmful to consumers, but the tone set by the Bureau permeated down to state regulators and even private plaintiffs' lawyers, with significant litigation, regulation and increased costs for the industry to meet the compliance demands of this climate.

I think it's fair to say the Trump administration emphasized cutting back on regulation, which led to a de-emphasis on consumer protection. This was apparent in the CFPB's switch from "regulation by enforcement" to more of a focus on consumer education and establishing rules with more clarity for the industry to live by.

As I'm writing this article in December of 2020, it's already apparent that consumer protection will again be en vogue. Senator Elizabeth Warren appears to carry a lot of clout in the new administration and her impact will be felt at the CFPB and beyond. In Congress, Representative Maxine Waters is already calling for the House Financial Service Committee to do more to protect consumers from the economic impact of Covid-19 and has been very harsh in her criticism of what she believes to be the CFPB's failure to protect consumers.

In the early days of the Covid-19 crisis, former Director Cordray sent a letter to Director Kraninger encouraging the CFPB to take action to protect consumers, including moratoriums on repossession, and encouraged oversight of servicing and collection activities such as forbearance and accommodations and challenged the Bureau to collect data on servicing metrics like hold time and call volume. I think it's fair to say we can anticipate robust activity on this front.

During the Obama years, the CFPB was the agency that flexed its muscles, but in the Trump administration the Federal Trade Commission (FTC) took a more active approach, perhaps to make up for the CFPB's perceived leadership vacuum. This was also apparent at the state level, with many state regulators and attorneys general becoming more aggressive, and several states creating their own many CFPB like agencies. This time around, I don't see these states stepping back due to a resurgence from the CFPB, instead, I see a potential "perfect storm" from federal agencies all the way down to the state regulators.

I question whether the Debt Collection rules that were recently published by the CFPB will ever take effect, as I think it is likely that a new Director will want to re-examine some of the provisions that have been criticized by consumer advocates such as number of contacts allowed and the clear distinction between first and third party collections. If you remember correctly, the CFPB under Director Cordray appeared to be blurring those lines and I fear that may be the case again.

Both Senator Warren and Representative Waters have attacked creditors' use of mandatory arbitration clauses as being harmful to consumers, and I expect a renewed attack on that front. In fact, the consumer advocacy group the National Consumer Law Center (NCLC) has published this as one of its federal priorities for 2021. As I write this, the two Georgia run-off elections for their Senate seats are still a month away. A Republican sweep of those seats would make a legislative attack on arbitration less likely, but a Democratic sweep, or even a split, makes that position somewhat tenuous.

Senator Warren and others have also been proponents of passing legislation that requires repair of vehicle recall items prior to sale. Again, this is on the NCLC's list of federal priorities for the coming year. This will be another area to keep an eye on and I expect to see the consumer advocates push in this direction and the impact on independent car dealers would be dramatic.

The affordability of vehicle payments and a customer's ability to repay will again be under scrutiny by the CFPB and I expect a renewed push in this area. What makes this issue so dangerous is that the last time around, the Bureau never offered meaningful guidance on a standard, it just seemed to attack what some in the industry were failing to do. Likewise, the pricing of both vehicles and after-market add-ons is likely to be another area of emphasis, as it seems that many consumer advocates almost view any profit as inherently abusive.

Finally, Covid-19 will continue to have a major impact on our justice system. Once the backlog in the courts is cleared, I expect to see heavy litigation from plaintiffs' lawyers, who've been forced to be on the sidelines for much of 2020. I expect that they'll be eager to get cases in front of sympathetic juries that have experienced this crisis themselves and may take a more harsh view of actions by creditors.

So what's the best course of action for independent dealers, finance companies and other creditors to take in this new climate? Check back next issue and I'll share some ideas.

2021 AND THE ROAD AHEAD - PART 2

Increased Regulation and Enforcement is Upon Us. What Does George Harrison Have to Do with Your Preparation?

In my previous article I discussed how the Biden Administration will impact the auto finance industry with increased regulation and a much more aggressive stance on consumer protection. Next, I'm going to present some ideas on steps you can take to protect your business and mitigate compliance risk over the next few years. Oddly enough, the inspiration for my message comes from George Harrison of The Beatles.

I've spent the past several months trying to talk folks off of the proverbial roof. The Democrats in positions of power, President Biden, Vice-President Harris, Senator Warren, Congresswoman Waters, all have made statements indicating we'll see more robust CFPB, and the track record of newly nominated CFPB Director Chopra certainly suggests a quick return to the dark days of "regulation by enforcement" of former Director Cordray. While there is certainly ample reason for concern, everyone needs to accept the current reality and prepare for this increased scrutiny.

The challenge, though, is that it's easy to put things off. Let's face it, compliance isn't a sexy topic for most, and its concepts can be a bit foreign. It's a lot more fun to talk about search engine optimization and selling cars than it is to discuss implementing a compliance management system. Then there's the fact that tax season begins soon after the New Year, so several companies take an "I'll do it later" and reassure themselves it's okay to wait until May. I've heard that lots of times before, and my observation is that when May comes, it will almost be time for summer vacations, and then back to school season, and then the holidays and year end are quickly upon us, the result being that the worthy aspiration of protecting the business will be repeatedly delayed.

That's where George Harrison comes in. While my favorite song of his is While My Guitar Gently Weeps, one can make a pretty good argument that his most beautiful lyrics were in his song Something. And that's my message to you well intentioned procrastinators. Do SOMETHING! Don't wait until next month or quarter. Do "something" today. Then build upon it perpetually, and pretty soon you'll be heads and shoulders above where you began. But you've got to choose to do SOMETHING and get started.

"Something" doesn't have to be a paradigm shift. In fact, I'd rather it not be, because the odds of sticking to it are much better if you take incremental steps rather than one big one. So let's start with some basics: When was the last time you had a qualified legal or compliance expert take a look at your deal jackets? If it's been more than a year then it's time to do it again. We conduct a lot of these reviews and I can't remember the last time I didn't have meaningful suggestions for material improvements. Your deal paperwork is the first thing that lawyers and regulators will look at, so get your house in order.

Next, make sure your personnel have a strong process for handling customer complaints. Every lawsuit against a dealer starts out as a complaint that was escalated due to non-resolution and every complaint to a regulator is only escalated after the customer didn't make progress with the company. In fact, the law books are filled with big dollar verdicts against car dealers that started out as minor matters that could have been resolved for small repairs or a refund. Adopt strong complaint management by keeping track of the complaints that come in, make sure your personnel have the tools to resolve them, and be proactive and look for common issues that repeatedly arise.

Another good strategy is to take the time to audit and examine your collection tactics. Make sure your written policies are in place and provide regular training to your collection personnel. In my opinion, twice a year is a reasonable training schedule for a collections department of just about any size, and that may even be conservative if there is high turnover. I think it's a good practice to grade a few calls per collector per month, and document when corrective action needs to be taken. I know this takes time and commitment, but it will take a whole lot less time than having to defend yourself later.

While we're talking about training, this would be a really good year to adopt a comprehensive training schedule for your company. This sounds intimidating but really isn't. Just about any creditor should be providing training on such global topics as information security and identity theft for all employees, and that training should be supplemented by job specific training on subjects like complaint management, underwriting, credit furnishing, sales and repossessions. Break out the calendar and come up with one training initiative per month. That spreads out the time so that your personnel won't get overwhelmed, while meeting the worthwhile objective of developing a demonstrable training program to support your compliance efforts.

Finally, give thought to having an actionable compliance management program. This has been preached for over a decade now, but I still see plenty of folks that either don't have a comprehensive program, or else they have a written program that is so ambitious that they can't possibly execute it. For those that need a refresher, your compliance program should include aspects of management oversight of compliance, written policies, training, complaint management, and audit. Again, you don't have to build this overnight, but establish a goal each month for spending some time on one of these functions. That effort gets aggregated and pretty soon you've got a real program.

I'll get off of my soapbox for now. You get the idea. You don't have to do it all, but do SOMETHING every week and every month, and those efforts will add up! Thanks for reading, good luck, and feel free to reach out if you'd like to discuss your specific situation and challenges.

ABILITY TO REPAY: WHOSE RESPONSIBILITY IS IT?

When I was in law school I clerked for a law firm that represented banks, which at the time, were enduring a wave of commercial litigation under the theory of so-called "lender liability". Banks would sue a borrower for failing to pay back a loan, and then the borrower would counter-sue the bank, arguing that it shouldn't have made these loans in the first place based on the customer's financial situation and that the bank treated the customer unfairly and otherwise took advantage of them. Sometimes the borrower wouldn't even wait to default and be sued and would instead sue the bank first. The legal proceedings that followed sought to excuse the debt and even hold the banks liable for additional damages, often in exorbitant amounts. The result of these lawsuits depended heavily on the specific facts of each case, which was very expensive to determine and involved lots of pre-trial discovery, so the lawyers got rich and many banks ended up on the losing end of verdicts.

In the past few years I've thought about these lender liability cases each time a state regulator or the CFPB brings up the concept of "ability to repay" and suggests that car dealers and finance companies should somehow bear responsibility for the inability of their customers to repay their car notes. I was of the impression that the CFPB was gearing up its pursuit of this theory in 2016 during the Director Cordray's leadership, but that died down under the new Bureau leadership which coincided with the Trump administration. Given the pronouncements that Director Chopra has previously made about the auto finance industry, I do fear that this theory will once again be pursued at the federal level.

At the state level, the regulators of Massachusetts have been very active against auto finance companies over the past several years, viewing industry practices as predatory, and have raised arguments that sound a lot like lender liability. It has obtained large settlements from Exeter Finance, Santander and, most recently, Credit Acceptance Corporation ("CAC"), among others. The 2020 action against Credit Acceptance Corporation included allegations that the company made high interest loans that it should have known its customers would be unable to repay, which resulted in customers losing their vehicles, down payments, and suffering other damages. Similar claims were previously made against others, including both Exeter and Santander. The CAC matter was resolved in September of 2021, with the company entering into $ 27 million settlement while admitting no wrongdoing.

So how does this relate to the independent car dealer? Well, for starters, dealers that originate retail installment contracts or leases are providing financing and are the original creditor to the transaction, whether they then hold and collect on the accounts themselves or sell them to another "indirect" lender such as a bank, credit union or finance company. This same argument about "knowing a customer would be unable to repay" can be made against the dealer.

Independent dealers that place their paper with indirect finance companies are certainly in the crosshairs for the "ability to repay" attack. They are the ones that structured the transaction and it could be argued that they are concerned with how much they'll make when they sell the contract and not how it will perform in the future. They've also been attacked for falsifying income to make the deals more appealing for the indirect lender, which results in damages to the consumer.

The argument may seem a bit more difficult to make against the buy here - pay here dealer that keeps the contracts and, thus, the risk, but Massachusetts took action against such a dealer a few years ago and brought the argument that the dealer's budget worksheet that it used to help consumers understand the impact of the proposed car note on their budget was faulty and was part of an underwriting process that underestimated the consumer's expense and costs in order to qualify them for loans they couldn't afford, to their detriment. The state won on its summary judgement motion in front of the court, and later the matter was settled with a consent decree in which the dealer paid $ 1.5 million in restitution and agreed to change practices.

In analyzing the potential risk faced by the dealer, it's important to keep in mind that state consumer protection laws are usually nebulous and broadly worded, and it wouldn't be a stretch for a consumer lawyer to include allegations similar to the ones found in the Massachusetts actions. While they are at it, the dealer could also be attacked for not having a strong enough underwriting policy, for not following it, or for making so many exceptions that one could argue no controls existed and that the consumer suffered as a result.

I know a lot of you feel like Alice in Wonderland right about now and think you've fallen through the rabbit hole. In all my years of advocating on behalf of the auto finance industry, I've never known a creditor that went into a transaction with the intent that the customer is going to default. That's not the way to have a sustainable business model, it ignores both the economic realities of your business and the risk you take putting "metal on the road".

I'm here to tell you, though, that's not the way some regulators think. In the Santander matter, the State of Massachusetts argued that the company didn't have a reasonable basis to believe that many accounts would be repaid and used the company's own analytics against it to argue that the company could predict default in certain credit bands. Based on my experience, I think it's more accurate to say that while statistical modeling can accurately predict default rates among a pool of accounts sharing similar characteristics, it can't predict how any specific account within such a group will behave.

Unfortunately, the zealous consumer advocates seem to have a predisposition to infer bad intent on the part of the creditor. Not to get sidetracked, but if the industry did stop providing credit in certain bands based on performance, it's not a stretch to predict that the industry would soon be fending off claims that it isn't making enough credit available to folks in those bands?

Going back to my first experiences with lender liability cases, I have a difficult time accepting the theory, probably because it places all responsibility on the creditor and not the borrower. There are certainly situations, such as with misrepresentation or deception, where the creditor bears responsibility; however, in my mind the most significant flaw in the "ability to repay" argument ignores the customer's own responsibility.

Assuming that the key transaction terms are disclosed to the customer (that's the purpose of Truth-In-Lending laws), then the customer is making the informed decision to proceed with the purchase and financing of the vehicle. In fact, the lengthy deal jackets that are common today are the result of the industry's attempt to keep up with "regulations gone wild" and cover all its bases and make sure the customer is informed. Isn't it then the customer's corresponding responsibility to evaluate its financial situation as a whole, study the terms of the transaction, and determine whether performance can be achieved? Let's face it, many customers enter into these transactions thinking in the short term and ignoring the fact that the contract extends for years. Again, that is the customer's failure and not the creditor's, and that fact shouldn't be ignored.

I don't mean to sound like an industry apologist, but I wish consumer advocates would focus on the concept of customer responsibility with as much gusto as they attack the industry. I am a zealous advocate for creditor education, training, and having adequate controls in place, all in an effort to make sure this industry has the knowledge necessary to succeed in its business while at the same time protecting itself. I'm also for the industry having a "fair shake" and "fighting chance", and I fear that by ignoring customer responsibility and apportioning the vast majority of responsibility to the creditor, that fairness is difficult if not impossible to achieve.

CHAPTER FOUR

What's Your Story?

Back when I was defending dealers and finance companies in lawsuits, I'd tell my clients that we had to be able to present a favorable story to the judge or jury. What I meant was that the plaintiff's lawyers would be doing everything possible to demonize my clients and portray them in a negative light. To combat that, we needed to be able to present a vastly different set of facts that demonstrate my clients were, in fact, good corporate citizens that did care about best practices and doing things right. When I transitioned my practice in the direction of keeping my clients from getting sued and out of trouble, these same rules applied. These articles in this chapter are a collection of suggestions on how to demonstrate a commitment to compliance and demonstrating a favorable story to a judge, jury or regulator if the need ever arises.

PUT YOUR TEAM IN A POSITION TO WIN

"How are you going to help me protect my business"? That's the question a prospective client recently asked me. I was impressed with this query because it quickly gets to the crux of why Ignite should be hired. This interview was a bit different than many I do, because this dealer was thinking ahead. Instead, I usually speak to folks that only want to address a specific issue that's on their mind that day, with no regard for the bigger picture, and if

I bring up the broader issues they think it's an attempt to expand the project or justify our services.

Without hesitation, I told this person that teaching his people how to spot and address risk is the most effective contribution I will make to protect his BHPH operation. To back up my assertion, I provided a few examples of that are pretty common:

- Identifying traps and tricks in credit dispute letters
- Spotting a dangerous fact pattern in a consumer bankruptcy case
- Teaching sales personnel about the difference between extended service contracts and limited warranties
- How to write more effective (and less risky) collection letters
- Setting up an effective complaint management system
- Walking dealership personnel through the Buyer's Guide, Credit Application, Retail Installment Contract and other documents used in the sale and financing of a vehicle.

Each of these issues could prove costly if mishandled, either through lawsuits or regulator action, and this is certainly not an all-inclusive list, it's just a short sampling of actual issues that I've dealt with recently. On this list alone there are about ten vastly different laws that could put a dealership in jeopardy and, again, that's just for starters. Failing to handle any one of them correctly could create costly liabilities.

Unfortunately, my observations in over 30 years of serving this industry is that training is often either ignored altogether or delivered in a "check the box" format which is woefully inadequate. Most training focuses on a high level overview of the "black letter law" rather than providing a practical understanding of how to work through a given issue. For instance, the vast majority of collection training I've seen provided to auto dealers and finance companies focuses on the Fair Debt Collection Practices Act ("FDCPA"), which is a federal law that applies to third parties collecting debt and provides an exemption for those collecting their own accounts (first party collectors). While it's true that many state laws have adopted similar provisions to the FDCPA that need to be understood, the end result of this training is often a focus on learning code sections not even applicable to the business. Even worse, many written policies state a goal of FDCPA compliance, which can then be used against the company if it falls short of achieving this goal.

My challenge to each one of you is to ask yourselves whether you are providing your personnel with sufficient training and context to do their jobs! I spoke to a bankruptcy account manager recently that had no previous experience handling bankruptcy cases and was moved into this position because someone else had left the company. Similarly, I recently trained an underwriting team that didn't know the difference between the Fair Credit Reporting Act ("FCRA") and Equal Credit Opportunity Act ("ECOA"), and I met with collectors that were never taught the proper message to leave on an answering machine and the dangers of saying too much. I could go on, but you get the idea.

You are depending on your personnel to make good decisions that will protect the company, but as sports coaches always say, "have you put the players in a position to win"? Has your team been provided with the tools to analyze the types of issues that come across their desk on a daily basis? Training doesn't (and shouldn't) need to take the form of a mini-law school class, but it should combine sufficient depth to understand the law or regulation with an examination of how these issues are likely to arise.

When I begin working with a new client, I often start by telling the personnel that I'm deputizing them to be my eyes and ears in identifying and eliminating compliance and legal risk. I'm not there every day, but they are, and they are in the best position to spot the issues and ask for help. If they can effectively identify the issues that need attention, we can then work together to handle them and protect the business. So look around your business with a fresh set of eyes and consider whether each department has received sufficient training to perform this function. If not, it's time to get started.

USE TRAINING TO PROPEL YOUR BUSINESS

Quality training is needed to maximize the performance of personnel and protect your businesses, but I think the combination of limited resources and the daily pressures and distractions of the business make achieving an adequate training plan a struggle. That's unfortunate, because it is my belief that there is a strong correlation between achieving great business results and providing top notch training to personnel that allows them to propel as well as protect the business. That should be all the incentive you need to address your training efforts.

Leadership Must Communicate the Importance it Places on Training

A quality training program doesn't have to be expensive or terribly complex. I've seen plenty of strong programs that were neither, and conversely, I've seen expensive programs that did little to provide meaningful education. One thing that all strong training programs have in common, though, is leadership commitment from the top, so let's start there. Ownership and senior management must embrace and communicate the importance of training to all employees. If the owner makes it known that training is a priority then personnel will take it seriously.

Provide Adequate Training in All Areas

Next, its' critical to identify what training to provide. The company has to take an honest approach, look at all functions of the business, and assess whether there is already formal training in place and whether certain areas aren't getting needed attention. A mistake I often observe is falling victim to a training imbalance, where a company will only train personnel on certain aspects of the business. For instance, I once had a client that loved buying and selling cars, and he'd gladly provide training to his team on how to do both. He was not comfortable handling collections, though, and never devoted enough attention or resources to collection training, which had a lot to do with his excessive default rates and closing of his store. Don't be guilty of this mistake; instead, take a holistic view of the business and evaluate whether there is sufficient training being provided in each area.

Identify the Right Trainers

Identify the strengths and weaknesses of your team and determine whether your managers/leaders have the skillset to conduct the training or whether outside expertise is needed. In my experience, dealerships have a lot of knowledge on things like underwriting, selling cars, and collections, but maybe not so much when it comes to compliance issues, so carefully assess whether the subject matter expertise is possessed in house or whether outside resources are needed. Just as important, ask whether the subject matter experts have the talent to communicate their message and work with others. We've all seen people that are very strong at their jobs, but lack the skill to pass that knowledge on to others.

Training Schedule

Once these questions have been addressed, a training schedule should be put in place. I don't think there is a magic formula here, but I think it is fair for employees to expect to be provided with training on their key job functions on an annual basis, and more frequently in departments that carry heightened risk or deal with customers or the public on a regular basis. Please keep in mind that when I talk about a training schedule I'm referring to formal training where time is set aside, materials may be provided, and participation is recorded. This is different than, but works to reinforce the "hands-on" training that should be happening daily/weekly/monthly within your organization.

In my mind, a good goal is to schedule training throughout the year, spread out among different departments, so that the time requirements of any single department would be minimal. Seriously, we're talking about an hour or so every three or four weeks, spread out among departments! Even the busiest dealers can make that commitment. Of course, practical considerations have to take priority. For instance, I don't try to schedule any training during tax season, nor do I like scheduling training between Thanksgiving and New Years. I'd also never try to schedule collections training near month-end. Those are simply my thoughts, and you may have some preferences of your own. Look at your own operations and functions and create a plan that fits your needs.

Conclusions

A robust training program IS within your grasp. With it, you'll make your employees more efficient, manage and reduce your compliance risk and make your business stronger and hopefully more profitable. A huge paradigm shift isn't necessary, but it will take a commitment to the program that filters from the top down throughout the company, and an honest assessment of what expertise exists in house and how to fill in the gaps with outside resources. Good luck, and feel free to reach out if you'd like more guidance.

WHAT CAN A COMPLIANCE MANAGEMENT SYSTEM DO FOR YOU?

Conference season is upon us and there will be no shortage of legal and compliance content. One area where I've noticed a gap between conference curriculum and the routine issues that dealers confront is on the subject of dealers' implementing a Compliance Management System (CMS). While the show presentations highlight the CFPB regulatory mandate that it expects businesses to have a CMS, less attention is paid to the numerous practical reasons that dealers need to invest in one. This is unfortunate, because in addition to being a regulatory requirement, there are lots of other benefits of a CMS.

The CFPB has set forth four components of a robust CMS. They are: 1) Executive Oversight; 2) Compliance Program; 3) Complaint Management; and 4) Audit. First, I will provide a quick overview of each, and then I'll illustrate the practical benefits to the business.

Executive Oversight of Compliance

The role of Executive Oversight is to have an informed management team that takes an interest in compliance and sets the expectation for the entire company. That sounds reasonable enough, but often proves to be elusive because management may not always understand how or where compliance applies and doesn't prioritize it; therefore, neither does the rest of its personnel.

Management has to set forth the expectation that rules will be followed. Is there someone in charge of compliance (Chief

Compliance Officer) or is nobody accountable? Do the leaders inform the employees of important compliance issues facing the industry or do they let them operate in a vacuum? Are violations corrected or swept under the rug if shortcuts are profitable?

If the owner or general manager tolerates a compliance lapse, then everyone else will, too. If, on the other hand, they prioritize compliance by frequently mentioning it and correcting mistakes when they are observed, the message will flow from the top down to everyone else. Once this is systematic, the importance of compliance will be recognized by all and the business will be less risky and more efficient.

The benefits of executive oversight are numerous, but the bottom line of business is to make money, and dealerships with executive involvement are in a better position to do so because they identify and limit risk. Leaders that are "hands on" and informed of the compliance dangers that exist can educate their personnel, monitor performance, and take corrective action when necessary. Owners, board members and those in similar positions of power should require that information on compliance topics flow to them so that they can measure performance. Profits can be threatened by just one or two failures in this area, so leaders need to view the business from a compliance perspective in addition to units sold and dollars collected.

A Compliance Program that "Walks the Walk"

This section is where the rubber meets the road. Are there policies (the rules) and procedures (how the rules are executed and followed) that govern the way you do business or not? Are employees trained so following policy becomes a part of the dealership's language and mores, or are they viewed as a nuisance and only begrudgingly mentioned? The biggest mistake dealers make is that they think they can buy compliance, put it on a shelf and gain the benefit of some magic cloak of invincibility! WRONG! You can't just "talk the talk", you've got to "walk the walk".

That means not merely buying generic policies. Instead, have policies that apply to the specific way the dealership conducts business. Be proactive and train all employees on the policies that touch upon their jobs, document the training, and take corrective action when necessary, and document such action.

I'm often asked to name the magic number of policies needed. There is no set number, it all depends on the business methods and practices. The dealer selling 20 units a month will have different needs than one selling 200 vehicles out of multiple locations. The key is to objectively look at how business is conducted and identify the relevant laws that must be obeyed and whether there are currently policies in place that demonstrate your commitment to follow these laws.

A company that takes this component seriously will be able to withstand regulatory or legal scrutiny when things go wrong or mistakes are made. Such a company will be able to demonstrate that it tries to operate the "right way", and any single instance of failure is isolated and not an indication of a widespread problem. That's important when having to defend oneself, because allegations of intentional indifference can prove costly.

Complaint Management and Resolution

Customer complaints provide critical insight into the business and opportunities for improvement. Well run companies don't ignore complaints, they examine them and use them to get smarter. Some customer issues are simply misunderstandings, while others provide notice of compliance issues that can harm the company. Therefore, it's important that all matters be tracked and evaluated so that investigation is easy, commonality of issues can be discovered, and records of resolution can be kept.

Again, not all dealerships will manage their complaints the same way. Larger businesses may buy software and complex resolution systems, while smaller dealerships may simply keep a spreadsheet. Whatever tool is chosen, care should be exercised to consistently and objectively enter the information and evaluate the claims being made. If a mistake has been made, admit it and move on. Take advantage of training and learning opportunities for your team, and notate this has occurred so that the business can demonstrate its commitment to compliance.

A robust compliance management system acts as a scorecard for the entire company. Trends can be spotted, opportunities for employee training will become evident, and the company will learn a lot about the customer perception of the products and services it offers and even the performance of its third party service providers. A dealer could pay an expert thousands of dollars to conduct an operational assessment that won't come close in value to the information that can be discovered by thorough complaint management. If you don't track your complaints then start doing it. If you already do it but aren't studying the results, then pay more attention and reap the rewards.

Audit

This may be the prong that is most scary and misunderstood. Don't worry, nobody is saying to call in one of the big accounting firms. This component simply calls for an objective review of operations to ensure compliance and that policies are followed. Objectivity can be tricky, especially in smaller dealerships, given the many hats people wear and the close quarters folks often work in, so give some consideration to having someone on the outside (lawyer, consultant, etc.) come in and conduct the assessment.

For a smaller dealer, the basic audit that looks at a handful of current deals, past charge offs, and repossessions may be sufficient, along with evaluating any policies in place and whether the dealer can demonstrate they are obeyed. For a larger dealer, the scope may grow to include evaluation of servicing, credit reporting, and similar sophisticated functions such as sending of adverse action letters or whether closing files contain all signatures. Again, the size and sophistication of the business determines the scope, but any audit is better than no audit so leave fear behind and start looking with a more critical eye.

Auditing takes some work, but it's valuable as an inexpensive way to keep score, plus it is better to find your own mistakes rather than have them uncovered by a regulator or plaintiff's lawyer. Dealers are more than willing to put forth the effort to develop metrics to track dollars and the performance of sales and collections. Taking a similar approach to the operational aspects of the business will ferret out bad behavior and also identify opportunities for efficiencies and potential profits.

Final Thoughts

The past several years have seen an unprecedented call for the development of CMS' in dealerships. While much focus has been given to the regulatory perspective, this article, instead, focuses on the practical impact a CMS can make on the business. Both reasons are important, so for those of you sitting on the fence thinking you won't ever be the unlucky one drawing the regulator's "short straw", give thought to the practical gains a CMS can help you achieve, jump down from that fence, and take the next step!

MAKE IT YOUR POLICY TO HAVE WRITTEN POLICIES!

One of my hardest cases involved a client that had to produce its collection policies and procedures manual in a lawsuit. My client proudly presented me with a manual that was several inches thick. "Collection Department Policy Manual of XXY Finance" appeared right on the cover. So far so good, right? Well you can't judge a book by its cover. When I read through the manual I noticed that the front cover was the last time "XYZ Finance" appeared. Instead, the rest of the manual referred to "ABC Finance", which was the apparent author. When I confronted my client with this regrettable fact, he admitted that he pilfered the manual when leaving an old job and meekly asked "that's not a problem, is it"? After spending lots of money in attorney's fees and a less than favorable settlement, he learned the hard way that it sure was indeed a problem.

Car dealers are being constantly lectured about the importance of having strong written collection policies and procedures. Having them demonstrates an intent to do business the "right way" and allows the dealer to argue that any failure in following these policies are the result of carelessness. It's easy enough for lawyers and other compliance experts and consultants to preach, but it's a lot harder to actually accomplish. After all, car dealers are in the business of selling cars, not writing policy manuals. Luckily, I've read and drafted lots of them so here are my suggestions on how to get started:

The Source

The best way to create an effective policy manual is to work with experts that create these for a living. They will ask the right questions, learn your operations, and craft a product that fits your business while taking into account the important legal and compliance issues. That can cost a lot of money, though, and not everyone is in a position to make that kind of investment.

Therefore, I bet a lot of folks reading this column have done what my client did. They either got their policy manual from another company, or they became "internet lawyers" and searched Google until they found something that's "close enough". In truth, there is plenty of good content on the internet. The trick is to use it as a starting point and not just slap your name on it and think you are finished. Read through a few manuals and see how they are organized and what topics are covered. Then ask yourself how it fits your business and make it adapt.

Once a solid draft has been created, share it with managers or other leaders in the company and see whether it is close to the "realities" of your business. Finally, bounce it off a consultant, lawyer, or other professional before it's published. It's a lot cheaper to have a lawyer proofread it and make suggestions in certain areas than to have them start from scratch, and you'll gain their perspective and guidance on how to make sure the manual doesn't fly in the face of relevant laws.

What's the Right Length?

There is a pretty good debate among experts about whether more is better or less is more. I tend to lean on the "less is more" approach. The manual should be thorough enough to cover all of the relevant business processes, but not so large that an employee can't possibly grasp all of the content. I've seen more than one witness tripped up during a deposition or trial examination because there was simply too much content to remember. Remember, these are "best practice" guidelines, not an intricate instruction manual covering every last duty an employee may have. Those are job descriptions, which is a column for another day.

Content

It's important to strike a balance between practicality and the law. It's insufficient to simply say "We will follow the Fair Debt Collection Practices Act." That's a worthwhile aspiration, but it gives the reader no direction on how to do it. Likewise, I've seen manuals that recite the relevant laws and statutes, but don't provide instructions on how to apply the law to day to day business operations. I prefer a technique that says something like "We strive to follow the Fair Debt Collection Practices Act in our work environment. To do this we have our employees follow the following rules regarding communicating with customers…..".

Deciding What to Include

There is an unlimited amount of information available about q subject as broad as collections. How does one decide what to include and what to keep out? My best advice is to tailor the content to your business practices. For instance, Article Nine of the Uniform Commercial Code deals with repossessions, and includes self-help repossession and also addresses "strict foreclosure", where the creditor accepts the return of the collateral in full satisfaction of the debt. Unless you actually allow your customers the option of utilizing strict foreclosure, it has no place in your manual. I've seen collectors get glassy eyed trying to remember a litany of rules that have no practical application to their business. This is where passing the manual around as a draft, as I suggested above, has a lot of value because your employees that perform these tasks will point out where the proposed language deviates from reality.

Your employees are a key resource in this exercise. Ask them for guidance on how accounts are handled. Create flow charts that follow your various processes. Only then should you attempt to document each of the various stops along the path. I've seen many companies make the mistake of over-valuing consultants and under-valuing their own subject matter experts, often with unfortunate results.

Training and Testing

Your policy and procedures manual should work in concert with training and testing initiatives. It isn't enough to publish the material or put it on a shelf. The sophisticated company will then implement it through training and then have the employees take short tests to demonstrate their mastery of the information. This should then be put in each employees' personnel folder. These tests should be given at least once a year. They don't have to be too fancy, maybe ten or fifteen questions to make sure the employees have made the effort. This makes a powerful statement to your employees that these policies are part of your company culture.

IGNITE YOUR CUSTOMER RETENTION WITH A COMPLAINT MANAGEMENT SYSTEM!

While I've certainly spent enough time in these pages challenging many of the initiatives of the CFPB, I must confess that I do agree with the emphasis it has placed on how car dealers handle and respond to customer complaints and the need for a complaint management system. In the eyes of the Bureau, consumer complaints provide businesses with a good indication of institutional weaknesses and practices that create acrimony with its customers. In my mind, failing to adequately address a complaint tells the customer they aren't important and does damage to the relationship that can be irreparable. Unfortunately, though, a lot of dealers aren't sure how to go about developing and implementing a strong complaint management strategy so they make excuse after excuse for not having one. That's where I can help.

My role with Ignite Consulting gives me lots of opportunities to speak to and work with dealers from all around the country. In my experience, there is a great chasm on how dealers are responding to this challenge. I've heard some dealers tell me that just about every call they get from a customer can be classified as a "complaint" of some sort and that keeping track of them will bring business to a grinding halt, while I've had other dealers say that they don't receive any complaints. My bet is that the truth is someplace in the middle, but even if a particular dealer leans to one side or the other, they still need to document a policy, successfully implement it, and be able to demonstrate that it's being followed.

Define what constitutes a "Complaint"

When creating a written complaint management policy, the first task is to arrive at a reasonable definition of "complaint". I believe a lot of folks don't give sufficient thought to this question, which results in inconsistent treatment of customers and inefficient use of employees' time. In my opinion, a customer complaint is a communication submitted that expresses dissatisfaction with or suspicion of wrongful conduct by the dealer related to a customer's personal experience with a product or service. This straightforward definition mandates that dealers accept responsibility for actions it's taken but isn't so broad as to include any event under the sun. I propose this as a starting point for the discussion but the specific business model and product and services offered will ultimately dictate the final definition.

Tell Customers How to Provide Feedback

Next, the written policy should establish that the dealer will give its customers clear direction on how to submit a complaint. If customers know where to go, they are more likely to communicate with the dealership and not reach out to social media, the local Better Business Bureau, lawyers, or the many other outlets available to them. I suggest presenting the information early in the relationship, in the welcome letter or other first communication with the customer. I also like having multiple avenues available, such as a dedicated email address and a portal on the website. I favor having the name and email address of the person that handles complaints posted at the dealership, too, though some clients push back and say that making this information readily available increases the number of complaints.

Track Complaints like any other Key Business Activity

The ability to track complaints is key, so referencing this capability should find its way into the policy. Whether it's a simple spreadsheet, an off the shelf customer relationship product, or a specific complaint management product, it should be comprehensive enough to compile all of the key information on the complaint, its handling, and resolution, if any. Having this information readily available gives the dealer the ability to look beyond anecdotal information and accurately analyze the business. If it can be tied into the Dealer Management System (DMS) that's even more efficient because it will save employees the step of having to add information twice.

Search for Common Issues

A key part of complaint tracking is the ability to identify common problems because it is a quick way to identify areas of weakness, challenges with an employee, and opportunities to improve customer service. It's up to the individual dealer to decide how granular this analysis should go, but topics like collection practices, credit reporting, repair issues, payment disputes, vendor specific complaints, repossession issues, and allegations of discrimination are a good place to start taking a deeper look. By rising above the allegations of any one customer and, instead, looking at the experience of the broader customer base, the dealer will gain a new understanding into how its business is perceived.

Identify Meaningful Metrics

Another vital component of complaint tracking is the ability to track how complaints are handled and responded to. Key areas to measure include days to first response, days open, complaints resolved upon initial communication, and complaints resolved are all metrics that give meaningful feedback on the effectiveness of the process being followed. Each business model presents its own unique set of challenges so be proactive and seriously consider what information provides the most insight to your own set of circumstances.

Complaint Resolution

Finally, good complaint management means keeping track of how complaints are resolved. That doesn't just mean if an accommodation was made or if money or a credit was given, because many problems can be solved without doing so. I think there is a tendency to focus on the problem accounts and not the complaints that were easily resolved. This results in a lot of "good" information being lost and never making its way to a report. This is unfortunate, because a significant number of complaints are minor and get handled to the customer's satisfaction. Unless this information is captured, though, the dealer won't be able to demonstrate this positive history to a regulator and is instead left with a skewed result.

Embrace a Culture of Compliance

The aforementioned process must be built upon a foundation that emphasizes excellent customer service and a culture that wants to retain its customers. Every dealership should appoint a Chief Compliance Officer and this person must be empowered to take action. In smaller dealerships that may be the owner or general manager while larger dealerships might have a dedicated person handling this role. In either case, the CCO should make sure the policy is written down, then develop training materials so that personnel are properly informed and educated, and then implemented throughout the company. Any employee that may be in a position to have a complaint communicated by a customer should receive this training. This strategic approach allows the dealer to build a "culture of compliance" that emphasizes the proper handling of customer complaints.

Conclusions

This is a pretty straightforward approach to establishing a Complaint Management System and can be acted upon today. Consideration must be given to the individual business model and products and services when creating this written policy and building a system. Don't just think about this article and then set it aside. Instead, pledge to take action. Whether it's reviewing the policy you already have in place, thinking about new ways to measure success in complaint tracking, or creating a new training initiative, get started today. Giving attention to this subject will increase the efficiency of your personnel, give you new insights into your business, and ultimately help you retain customers.

CHAPTER FIVE

Information Security

For several years, I've believed that information security is a risk to which most finance companies and dealers don't pay enough attention. Remember what I said about folks not wanting to spend on compliance? I think that same reluctance exists when it comes to investing in information security. How important is this? I've included a chapter on this vital subject, that's how much! I want to thank Robbie Hudson (Richard's twin brother) for providing me lots of education on this subject during his time with Ignite.

WHO CAN YOU TRUST TO PROTECT YOUR DATA?

In the past year I've spent a good deal of ink writing about both the importance of data security and the critical task of vendor selection. Unfortunately, those issues have once again collided, as it's recently been reported that the fast food chain Wendy's suffered a significant data breach which has resulted in inconvenience to lots of customers, bad press, and some class action lawsuits.

What does a burger chain's problems have to do with car dealers? No, I'm not comparing your inventory to chopped meat, but this subject has everything to do with your business because whether you're selling cars or burgers, you're likely accepting credit card payments and, therefore, you're taking possession of and probably storing your customers' personal information. In doing so you're working with third party vendors, which apparently is the way that hackers were able to thwart Wendy's data security protections and wrongfully obtain its customer information.

What Constitutes Good Data Security?

As I've previously published in these pages, good data security for independent car dealers involves a combination of buying and then implementing the right technology, having the right policies and procedures for employees to follow and then making sure that they do so, and having the right facility security such as clean desk policies, door locks and control of areas that contain customer information. This is a vast oversimplification, but a good place to start as a frame of reference.

How to Prioritize Your Vendor Scrutiny

While there is no foolproof way to guard against a vendor's security lapse leaving your data vulnerable, there are a lot of practices you can follow to weed out the less stringent vendors, thereby facilitating your selection of vendors that are up to speed on the risks involved and committed to security. Keep in mind that even though this article focuses on technology vendors, a vendor is anyone with whom you do business, which could include a wide range of service providers like those you use for mass mailing of letters, software providers, repossession companies, and a whole host of others, and these same practices can be utilized as part of a comprehensive vendor management strategy.

Not all vendors are created equal. Some, like a dealer management software supplier, provide crucial services that allow you to run the business, while others touch a much smaller aspect of the business. The costs and time involved in the vendor management program can be staggering, so some decisions have to be made as to where to devote resources. A lot of this has to do with the size and complexity of the business, and a dealer with one location selling a few dozen cars a month doesn't have to devote the same resources as a multi-location dealer selling hundreds.

So how does a dealer analyze the totality of its vendors and decide where to focus its resources? As a matter of simplicity, the important things to consider are:

a. Does the vendor have access to your customer data?

b. Does the vendor have access to your physical location?

c. Does the vendor provide key services or involve a significant financial commitment?

d. Does the vendor regularly have direct contact with your customers?

Those that fall into these categories present more of a risk to your business and should be subject to more scrutiny than others that don't.

How to Select Vendors that are Serious about Data Protection

When it comes to development of a rigorous vendor selection process, consider these four steps:

Due Diligence is all about knowing the details of the company you are hiring. It involves finding out about the company itself, its owners, employees that will be providing services to you and your customers, and its history and reputation. Don't simply go by claims it makes in a brochure or base a decision on one or two references they provide. Ask them for five or ten clients you can contact and then choose one or two. Investigate its record with any appropriate regulators and on social media, look into any lawsuits it has been involved in, and ask about how it protects the reputation of its clients. Study their policies and procedures to make sure they share your commitment to compliance, and take a look at their hiring policies and how they train and discipline their employees.

Vendor Contracts govern the relationship between the parties and are usually one-sided documents drafted by the vendor and then signed by the client without further thought. I've seen plenty of these contracts that go so far as to attempt to place liability on the dealer even if it's the vendor that does something wrong. It's critical that expert advice be sought to level the playing field and create a fair document that both parties can live by. Again, don't be afraid to make the vendor warrant and represent the specific services that will be provided, set goals and standards, and include penalties for non-performance and even termination rights in the event of a vendor violation.

Audit Rights should be included in your vendor contracts, and dealers should then have a process in place to conduct these audits. Audits aren't as scary as the word sounds. For less critical vendors, the process is simply keeping an eye on the points studied during due diligence to make sure the status quo is being maintained. Where appropriate, it may include tracking performance metrics and whether any service level agreement is being obeyed. Keep a keen eye on how customer complaints are communicated and handled. It's important to develop a consistent process for audits, schedule them at least annually, and document your files.

Site Visits are important for those vendors that provide critical functions because they allow for insight into how business is really done. Don't be shy about getting your hands dirty. For example, listen to phone calls for customer support or call center vendors, observe the actual people that touch your accounts, and sit in on training. Ask to see examples of employee discipline and compare how accounts are actually being handled to the representations made in the contract or service level agreement. Maybe even send a survey to customers that had dealings with the vendor. While site visits can be expensive and should be based on the size and complexity of the businesses involved, they are a handy tool to protect one's interests.

Next Steps

Don't just dog-ear this page after reading it. The costs for a data breach can be staggering, ranging from fines and lawsuits to the costs of obeying all the legal requirements thrust upon a party that's been breached, to damage to your reputation and loss of customer loyalty. While there is no "bullet-proof" remedy available, following these basic recommendations will assist you in building your vendor management program and allow you to control your business relationships and reduce your risk.

Finally, recognize the value of a paper trail and the importance of being able to demonstrate your efforts. Have written policies and procedures, develop a methodology for vendor selection, train your people, audit your vendors, and self-audit yourself to make sure you are meeting your own standards. By doing these things you'll be able to prove you're serious about compliance and hold those you do business with to the same goals.

THERE'S MORE TO INFORMATION SECURITY THAN BUYING THE RIGHT TECHNOLOGY.

You've hired great IT people to set up your dealership network. You've bought the equipment they specified and installed the most up to date virus protection on your computers. You've even voraciously read every article you can find about how to defeat hackers. You think your business is protected and you'll never be the victim of a costly security leak and the myriad of problems that come with it! Guess again, because buying the right hardware and security tools are only part of the puzzle. Too often dealers focus on technology tools and forget about the basic "best practices" that can make or break the business. Instead, use this three prong attack to ensure that both your customers' sensitive personal information and your critical business data are protected.

Security of Facility.

The layout of the dealership presents lots of ripe opportunities for the compromise of information. One of the most common mistakes is information being open and available at the receptionist or other employee's desks, where customers, vendors, or other invitees can catch a glimpse or do worse. Thought should be given to what type of information is handled by employees that interact directly with the public, thus increasing the odds that visitors will be in proximity to documents they shouldn't see. More importantly, every dealership should have a "clean desk" policy which prohibits sensitive information from being kept on a desk when left unattended. Make sure that employees have access to locked drawers and file cabinets in which to store papers when stepping away from the desk. Even employees with offices should either have the ability to lock up their papers or their office.

Secondly, consider whether all employees have access to the entire facility, or whether access is restricted by job description so that employees aren't free to enter areas where they have no reason to go. In a larger dealership that handles both front end sales and collections, for instance, the front end employees wouldn't have much of a reason to have unfettered access to the collections department, nor would collections personnel have reason to freely walk through the accounting office. Those areas could be kept behind locked doors. In a smaller dealership, it may not be practical to restrict access, though, so it's important to consider proper placement of personnel and the other measures discussed herein.

Next, what policies and procedures are in place to limit the access of third party vendors such as delivery personnel, repairmen, and other service providers? Are they required to physically sign in and out when they come and go? Are they escorted back to the work area and supervised, or are they left to wander around the facility? What kind of due diligence is done to investigate these vendors?

Know who you are doing business with and make sure that they have policies and procedures in place to hire trust-worthy people before you let them into your business. Special attention should be given to cleaning crews and any other personnel that are given access to the facility after hours without supervision. For those sensitive positions, even more due diligence is appropriate, and it is not unreasonable to ask if those employees are bonded and what type of insurance is covered to protect the dealership in the event of wrongful conduct.

Don't choose convenience over security. They are both important. Put copy machines, fax machines and scanners behind locked doors. Put good shredders next to every waste paper basket. Understand where various employees need to go within the dealership and where access should be limited to those with a specific purpose. These are simple steps that can eliminate problems.

Build a Culture of Security.

Employees, through careless or negligent conduct or through intentional acts, are probably the biggest point of vulnerability for a dealership. Protect your business by conducting robust pre-employment screening to make sure your future employees are trustworthy. On the first day of work (or as soon as possible if never done before) have employees sign a Confidentiality Agreement that sets forth how they are to handle confidential information they come across as an employee and restricts their use of such information in any capacity. Test the employees at least annually on their confidentiality obligations and, upon separation, provide them with a copy of the signed Agreement and remind them of their obligations under it.

Make sure to have an Employee Handbook that has sections dealing with information security and the expectations being placed upon them. Have a one page summary for them to sign and put it in their personnel file. Have a strong training program that includes education on security concerns and then test every employee on those standards and document the results in personnel files. This should be done at least annually and preferably more often so that employees understand the seriousness of the issue.

"Hot button" issues that should be referenced in these training materials include: What are the company policies regarding use of thumb drives, camera phones, and any other portable devices? Are employees allowed to access the internet while at work and, if so, is access restricted to certain sites? Are employees allowed to access their personnel email accounts while at work? Are employees allowed to email company information to their personal email accounts? Can employees download data, reports, or customer information to portable devices such as tablets and phones? The possible topics are extensive and will vary greatly depending on the size and type of business of the dealership. It's important, though, to consider these types of issues because your employees can literally carry your business in their pockets.

It is all too common that dealerships are vulnerable to an information breach upon the separation of an employee. A good way to protect the business is to have a sophisticated separation process that is systematic, routine, and applied consistently no matter the job description. Critical items should include a list of all parties that should be notified of the exit; list of all systems and programs to which employee has access; list of company property in their possession; disable system access and recover keys and badges; delete or redirect accounts, including VPN, network, email, and voicemail; removal from distribution lists; and notify vendors and clients as appropriate. Additionally, remember to provide the departing employee with a copy of the Confidentiality Agreement they signed during their employment and remind them of the serious consequences of any breach.

Make Technology Secure.

Congratulations, you've bought all of this technology to protect your business! Now it's time to make sure it doesn't do you harm. The first thing to do is check you have an appropriately sophisticated firewall for your business. This will keep the bad guys out of your system, or at least it should. Next, give thought to whether or not wireless access is provided. A lot of dealerships provide it as a convenience to its customers and employees; however, outsiders can connect to your system and that can be dangerous. If a stranger figures a way in, it can obtain an address within the system and information. It may be a good idea to turn off wireless access outside of business hours.

With more employees working from home, outside service providers like accountants looking for access, and even owners wanting easy access to reports at night and on weekends, remote access has become a big issue. Although expensive, a virtual private network ("VPN") is the safest option. Spend the extra money and get that extra level of security.

As previously stated, we allow our employees to carry the business in their pockets. Consider installing tracking tools on mobile devices such as phones, laptops and tablets. These allow for locating the device when missing, and can also be used to remotely wipe data from the device should the need arise. Also, consider what type of information employees are allowed to store on a device. Should sensitive reports and data be downloaded to a device that can be taken anywhere? Further, not all job descriptions are created equal. Some are much more sensitive than others and deserving of more sophisticated encryption technology being placed on their devices.

Next, take a good look at your policies and procedures related to employee use of email and the network. There should be a prohibition against using shared logins. Each employee should have a unique username so that their activities can be identified and they can be held accountable. All too often, employees share logins for convenience, especially if they do the same job. There should also be an aggressive password policy that requires it to be changed on a regular basis, such as monthly or quarterly. Have your IT folks create robust password criteria that require symbols, numbers and letters and doesn't allow the same password to be used repeatedly. Finally, have a policy that requires automatic screensavers after brief periods of inactivity, such as 10-20 minutes. Again, it's worth the small inconvenience to be assured that your computer stations won't be open when employees leave their desks for extended periods of time.

It's also important to educate your employees to the practical dangers presented in today's web based environment. Many aren't familiar with "phishing", "spoofing", and similar email attacks that can leave your entire network open to invasion and viruses. Provide training materials so that employees are on the lookout for fictitious emails and false web addresses. Give them the tools they need to act as your front line of defense, then test them to make sure that they understand the information.

Conclusions.

Long gone are the days of simply locking up the dealership at night. The same technology that allows dealers to be more efficient also presents a multitude of dangers. Acquiring the right tools is only part of the challenge and must be combined with having controls in place for both the facility and the employees that work there. Take the initiative and examine not only the policies and procedures that govern information security but also the practical aspects of how the dealership is run. By attacking all three of these prongs, a dealer can put itself in the best position to make sure its information and customers are protected.

IGNITE YOUR INFORMATION SECURITY PRACTICES

Over the last year, the Federal Trade Commission has taken a renewed interest in how businesses protect customer information. They've even published a booklet, Start with Security: A Guide for Business, to assist businesses to formulate their own strategies, which can be found at FTC.gov). This is a great resource because the FTC has created a list of tips for businesses to follow based on many cases it's pursued.

From talking to many independent dealers, though, it seems as if the message hasn't been heard. Too many of you think that good information security is simply a matter of buying the right equipment such as firewalls and virus protection. Guess again, because that's just a start, and simple things like a stolen device, employee negligence, or falling for a phony email are just as if not more likely as a cyber-attack to bring down your house of cards. It's important to remember that protecting both your customer's sensitive information and protecting your sensitive business data is the job of every employee. Perform a self-audit of the following three areas to see where things stand:

Technology – Good news and Bad news.

Virtually every dealer is dependent on technology to run their business. The efficiencies and other benefits are just too great but the bad news is that technology can also do harm unless a thoughtful approach to its use is taken. The first thing to do is check you have an appropriately sophisticated firewall. This will help keep hackers and other bad guys out of your system. Next, give thought to whether or not wireless access is provided on the premises. A lot of dealerships provide it as a convenience to its customers and employees; however, outsiders can connect to your system and that's dangerous. If a stranger figures a way in, it can obtain an address within the system and then have access to information. It's a good idea to turn off wireless access outside of business hours and audit access frequency.

With more employees working from home, outside service providers like accountants looking for access, and even owners wanting easy access to reports at night and on weekends, remote access has become a big issue. Although expensive, a virtual private network ("VPN") is the safest option. Spend the extra money and get that extra level of security.

Next, employees can carry your business in their pockets. It's a good safety precaution to have tracking tools installed on mobile devices such as phones, laptops and tablets. These allow for locating the device when missing, and can also be used to remotely wipe data from the device should the need arise. Having that ability can save you sleepless nights in the event a device goes missing. It's also important to look at your policy manual and see whether it addresses what type of information employees are allowed to store on a device. Does it address whether sensitive reports and data be downloaded to a device that can be taken anywhere? Are all employees subject to the same policies, or do employees that have access to more sensitive information prompted to use additional encryption tools?

It's also beneficial to examine policies and procedures related to employee use of email and software. There should be a prohibition against using shared logins. Each employee should have a unique username so that their activities can be identified and they can be held accountable. Frequently, employees share logins for convenience, especially if they do the same job or cover for one another due to vacations and other staffing needs. Make it your policy to have unique logins so that you have an audit trail of what actions were taken by each employee.

Do you have a password policy? I encourage use of an aggressive password policy that requires change on a regular basis, such as monthly or quarterly. Have your IT folks create robust password criteria that require symbols, numbers and letters and doesn't allow the same password to be used repeatedly. Finally, have a policy that requires employees to lock their computers if they leave their desk and use automatic screensavers after brief periods of inactivity, such as 5-10 minutes. A visitor to your location should never have access to sensitive information on a computer screen or access to your network because an employee failed to lock their computer.

Lastly, educate your employees to the practical dangers presented in today's web based environment. Many aren't familiar with "phishing", "spoofing", and similar email attacks that can leave your entire network open to invasion and viruses. Provide training materials so that employees are on the lookout for fictitious emails and false web addresses. Give them the tools they need to act as your front line of defense, then test them to make sure that they understand the information.

Facility Security – Does it allow access to sensitive information?

The layout of the dealership presents lots of ripe opportunities for the compromise of information. One of the most common mistakes is information being open and available at the receptionist or other employee's desks, where customers, vendors, or other invitees can catch a glimpse or do worse. Thought should be given to what type of information is handled by employees that interact directly with the public, thus increasing the odds that visitors will be in proximity to documents they shouldn't see. More importantly, every dealership should have a "clean desk" policy which prohibits sensitive information from being kept on a desk when left unattended. Make sure that employees have access to locked drawers and file cabinets in which to store papers when stepping away from the desk. Employees with offices should either have the ability to lock up their papers or their office.

Consider whether all employees have access to the entire facility, or whether access is restricted by job description so that employees aren't free to enter areas where they have no reason to go. In a larger dealership that handles both front end sales and collections, for instance, the front end employees wouldn't have much of a reason to have unfettered access to the collections department, nor would collections personnel have reason to freely walk through the accounting office. Those areas could be kept behind locked doors. In a smaller dealership, it may not be practical to restrict access, though, so it's important to consider proper placement of personnel and the other measures discussed herein.

Next, what policies and procedures are in place to limit the access of third party vendors such as delivery personnel, repairmen, and other service providers? Are they required to physically sign in and out when they come and go? Are they escorted back to the work area and supervised, or are they left to wander around the facility? What kind of due diligence is done to investigate these vendors?

Know who you are doing business with and make sure that they have policies and procedures in place to hire trust-worthy people before you let them into your business. Special attention should be given to cleaning crews and any other personnel that are given access to the facility after hours without supervision. For those sensitive positions, even more due diligence is appropriate, and it is not unreasonable to ask if those employees are bonded and what type of insurance is covered to protect the dealership in the event of wrongful conduct.

Don't choose convenience over security. They are both important. Put copy machines, fax machines and scanners behind locked doors. Put good shredders next to every waste paper basket. Understand where various employees need to go within the dealership and where access should be limited to those with a specific purpose. These are simple steps that can eliminate problems.

Employees can be a Threat

Employees, through careless or negligent conduct or through intentional acts, are probably the biggest point of vulnerability for a dealership. Protect your business by conducting robust pre-employment screening to make sure your future employees are trustworthy. On the first day of work (or as soon as possible if never done before) have employees sign a Confidentiality

Agreement that sets forth how they are to handle confidential information they come across as an employee and restricts their use of such information in any capacity. Test the employees at least annually on their confidentiality obligations and, upon separation, provide them with a copy of the signed Agreement and remind them of their obligations under it.

Make sure to have an Employee Handbook that has sections dealing with information security and the expectations being placed upon them. Have a one page summary for them to sign and put it in their personnel file. Have a strong training program that includes education on security concerns and then test every employee on those standards and document the results in personnel files. This should be done at least annually and preferably more often so that employees understand the seriousness of the issue.

"Hot button" issues that should be referenced in these training materials include:

- What are the company policies regarding use of thumb drives, camera phones, and any other portable devices?
- Are employees allowed to access the internet while at work and, if so, is access restricted to certain sites?
- Are employees allowed to access their personnel email accounts while at work? Are employees allowed to email company information to their personal email accounts?
- Can employees download data, reports, or customer information to portable devices such as tablets and phones?

The possible topics are extensive and will vary greatly depending on the size and type of business of the dealership.

Dealerships are especially vulnerable to an information breach upon the separation of an employee. A good way to protect the business is to have a sophisticated separation process that is systematic, routine, and applied consistently no matter the job description. Critical items should include:

- a list of all parties that should be notified of the employee's departure;
- list of all systems and programs to which employee has access;
- list of company property in their possession;
- disable system access and recover keys and badges;
- ·delete or redirect accounts, including VPN, network, email, and voicemail; removal from distribution lists; and notify vendors and clients as appropriate.

I also think it's a good practice to provide the departing employee with a copy of the Confidentiality Agreement they signed during their employment and remind them of the serious consequences of any breach.

Learn about Cyber-Liability Insurance

Be proactive and ask your insurance professional about obtaining cyber liability insurance to protect you in the event of an unfortunate episode. This type of insurance can save your business! If there is a data breach, most dealers are not prepared to incur significant costs that hit quickly such as legal and forensic services to discover a breach, regulatory compliance and notice of affected persons; customer credit monitoring, business interruption expenses, damage to your network and lost data, and a public relations campaign to control reputational damage. This type of insurance coverage is very valuable and it's important for the business leaders to understand how it is different from regular errors and omissions coverage and how it can be tailored to fit a particular business.

Conclusions

Dealers can no longer lock up the gates at night and feel that their business is protected. It's necessary to build controls for the facility, technology and the employees that work there. By attacking all three of these prongs highlighted in this article, a dealer can put itself in the best position to protect its information and that of its customers.

EMPLOYEES AND CYBERSECURITY RISK

Cyber-security has become an industry buzzword over the past few years, as data breaches have received publicity and companies have learned of the significant costs that accompany a breach. As a result, significant technology and other investments have been made to increase protections. Often, though, the vulnerabilities that employees present are overlooked. That is unfortunate, because they pose a significant threat that can't be fixed by throwing money and technology at the problem. The good news is that with a thoughtful approach and proper training, significant strides can be achieved.

While wrongful employee conduct such as theft and fraud certainly present a danger, many companies conduct background checks and have "on-boarding" procedures in place to weed out those bad actors. I certainly don't want to discount the danger of intentional bad actors, but in the limited space I have I'd instead like to focus on several of the opportunities for harm that can jeopardize a business from unintentional acts of employees.

Email Can Ruin Your Day!

Perhaps the biggest threat to security is the wide-spread and often uncontrolled use of email. For most companies, it's the lifeline of communication, but along with it comes the risk of ransom-ware, spoofing, phishing, viruses, and other technological "dark arts" that can bring business to a grinding halt. It isn't fancy, but companies can avoid these dangers with a training program to teach employees to avoid opening attachments from unknown sources, verify the identity of senders, and recognize legitimate email from a phishing one. My observation is that repetitive training is the key and I recommend initial training of all employees to identify the tricks and tools of hackers and other bad actors, quarterly email reminders to reinforce the material, and, for larger businesses, using an outside company to send "test" emails to ferret out susceptible employees.

Common Practices Regarding Technology

Next, it's important to examine the daily practices followed by employees, with the goal being to ferret out those habits that present risk. Examples include: whether the company regulates bring your own device ("BOD"); rules about use of thumb drives; rules about data classification and encryption of data; remote system access; guest system access; mobile device policy; sharing of passwords; and both physical and network security policies. There is both convenience and danger in each of these issues, and it is important to give thoughtful consideration to how these competing goals should be balanced.

Navigating the Fine Line of Policies

There is a fine line to walk between having sufficient, clear policies that set forth expectations regarding the aforementioned issues, and having too many policies that over-burden and confuse employees. It's critical that employees are able to execute on the policies that are in place. Put policies under the microscope and objectively evaluate whether they are easy to understand and put into everyday practice or whether they provide a false sense of security by "talking the talk", but make it difficult to "walk the walk". This can be especially dangerous because businesses are often forced to demonstrate their compliance to lawyers and regulators. A complicated policy that isn't followed can be twisted into a conclusion that the company was negligent or intentionally disregarded its own rules.

Audit System Access

It's important to have rules in place about accessing systems and regularly changing codes and passwords. Very often employees change jobs and areas of responsibility over time, but unless there are management rules in place, old program access is never changed. The result is employees end up with access to many systems they no longer need to perform the new job functions, and they maintain logins and codes that can be manipulated and exploited by wrongdoers. This can be resolved with regular auditing and eliminating access that is no longer necessary.

Likewise, there should be rules about mandatory changing of security codes and passwords to help ensure that computers, software, and related tools are only used by necessary personnel. Similarly, there should be clear rules about not keeping passwords and sensitive information located on keyboards or around the workstation, and regular inspections to guard against these practices. Measures like these are obvious, but there should be accountability to make sure they are performed.

Have an Off-Boarding Procedure

One frequently overlooked area of vulnerability is ex-employees. They often have "the keys to the kingdom" and great care should be given to construct a written "off-boarding" procedure that protects the company and is followed consistently. This is true whether separation is a result of forced termination or a voluntary departure.

First, consider who needs to be notified. Are there vendors, third party service providers, or even clients or customers that have regular communication with the soon to be ex-employee? Care should be given to let these parties know that the subject person is no longer with the company and is no longer authorized to conduct company business.

Another best practice that should be followed immediately upon hiring and throughout the term of employment, is to keep a list of all systems to which the employee has access and all company property in their possession, including serial numbers. This will allow for quick disabling of systems and recovery of company equipment. Portable devices contain a myriad of sensitive information and are often lost in the shuffle when technology is updated, so keeping this list will avoid confusion and having to endure the embarrassment of locating devices later.

Finally, be sure to immediately disable system access, especially any wireless or remote access, turn off all access to social media, and recover things like keys and badges. Social media has become an especially important issue because of the ease of access and immediate impact it makes, so be sure that restrictions are put in place. Include the rules and limitations on its use in an employee handbook.

Summary

Employees probably represent the biggest threat to a company's cyber-security. Just by doing their jobs, they have critical access to systems and regularly confront choices that affect the safety of the institution. Companies must balance the need for efficiency with the need for safety and proactively identify threats and take steps to protect themselves. Management should require its subject matter experts to implement training and education on these issues and document a plan to establish clear procedures.

HOW SECURELY DO YOU PROTECT YOUR CUSTOMER'S INFORMATION?

Too often dealers and finance companies focus on technology tools and forget about the basic "best practices" that can make or break the business. When it comes to the obligation to protect a customer's personal information, it's the failure to pay attention to the details that can get you in trouble. Use this guide to ensure that your customers' sensitive personal information and your critical business data are protected.

Security of Facility.

The layout of the dealership presents lots of ripe opportunities for the compromise of information. Thought should be given to what type of information is handled by employees that interact directly with the public, thus increasing the odds that visitors will be in proximity to documents they shouldn't see. Every dealership should have a "clean desk" policy which prohibits sensitive information from being kept on a desk when left unattended and employees should have access to locked drawers and file cabinets in which to store papers when stepping away from the desk.

Consider whether all employees should have access to the entire facility, or whether access can be restricted by job description so that employees aren't free to enter areas where they have no reason to go. Sale's personnel don't have much of a reason to have unfettered access to the collections department, nor would collections personnel have reason to freely walk through the accounting office. In a smaller dealership, it may not be practical to restrict access so it's important to consider proper placement of personnel and the other measures discussed herein.

Are there written policies and procedures in place to limit the access of third party vendors such as delivery personnel, repairmen, and other service providers? Are they required to physically sign in and out when they come and go? Are they escorted back to the work area and supervised, or are they left to wander around the facility? What kind of due diligence is done to investigate these vendors?

Don't choose convenience over security. They are both important. Put copy machines, fax machines and scanners behind locked doors. Put good shredders next to every waste paper basket. These are simple steps that can eliminate problems.

Build a Culture of Security.

Employees are probably the biggest point of vulnerability for a dealership so conduct robust pre-employment screening to make sure your future employees are trustworthy. Have all employees sign a Confidentiality Agreement that sets forth how they are to handle confidential information and restricts their use of such information in any capacity. Test the employees at least annually on their confidentiality obligations and, upon separation, provide them with a copy of the signed Agreement and remind them of their obligations.

Make sure to have an Employee Handbook that has sections dealing with information security and have a strong training program that includes education on security concerns and then test every employee on those standards and then document the results in personnel files. "Hot button" issues that should be referenced in these training materials include: What are the company policies regarding use of thumb drives, camera phones, and any other portable devices? Are employees allowed to access the internet while at work and, if so, is access restricted to certain sites? Are employees allowed to access their personnel email accounts while at work? Are employees allowed to email company information to their personal email accounts? Can employees download data, reports, or customer information to portable devices such as tablets and phones? Consider these types of issues because your employees can literally carry your business in their pockets.

Dealerships are vulnerable to an information breach upon the separation of an employee so have a sophisticated separation process that is systematic, routine, and applied consistently no matter the job description. Critical items should include a list of all parties that should be notified of the exit; list of all systems and programs to which employee has access; list of company property in their possession; disable system access and recover keys and badges; delete or redirect accounts, including VPN, network, email, and voicemail. Additionally, remember to provide the existing employee with a copy of the Confidentiality Agreement they signed during their employment and remind them of the serious consequences of any breach.

Make Technology Secure.

You've bought all of this technology to protect your business but make sure it won't do you harm. Check you have an appropriately sophisticated firewall for your business. This will keep the bad guys out of your system, or at least it should. Next, give thought to whether or not wireless access is provided. A lot of dealerships provide it as a convenience to its customers and employees; however, outsiders can connect to your system and that can be dangerous so it may be a good idea to turn off wireless access outside of business hours.

Consider installing tracking tools on mobile devices such as phones, laptops and tablets. These allow for locating the device when missing, and can also be used to remotely wipe data from the device should the need arise. Also, consider what type of information employees are allowed to store on a device. Not all job descriptions are created equal. Some are much more sensitive than others and deserving of more sophisticated encryption technology being placed on their devices.

Be sure to have policies and procedures related to employee use of email and the network. There should be a prohibition against using shared logins; each employee should have a unique username so that their activities can be identified and they can be held accountable. There should also be an aggressive password policy that requires change on a regular basis, such as monthly or quarterly. Have a policy that requires automatic screensavers after brief periods of inactivity, such as 10-20 minutes. Again, it's worth the small inconvenience to be assured that your computer stations won't be open when employees leave their desks for extended periods of time.

Conclusions.

The days of simply locking up the dealership at night are over. Take the initiative and examine not only the policies and procedures that govern information security but also the practical aspects of how the dealership is run. By attacking all three of these prongs, a dealer can put itself in the best position to make sure its information and customers are protected.

HOLLA BACK:

The Significance of the CFPB's Action against Dwolla

In its first action focusing on the subject of data security, in March of 2016 the CFPB recently entered into a consent decree with Dwolla, Inc., an online digital payment system that allows consumers to engage in bank transfers and, as part of its offering, collects and stores sensitive personally identifiable consumer information. This matter has important considerations for car dealers, particularly BHPH dealers that routinely collect electronic payments using third party vendors.

To truly understand the impact of this matter, it's critical to note that first, Dwolla isn't a huge player in the payments space, moving an estimated $ 5,000,000.00 per day, which may seem like a lot but is small compared to others. Secondly, there was no demonstration that a consumer actually suffered harm; instead, the action was based on representations Dwolla made. Think about that! The CFPB didn't wait for a consumer to suffer damages or even complain. It took action because of statements made by the company, either on its website or in communications with consumers, such as:

- Dwolla is PCI Compliant;
- "100% of your information is encrypted and stored securely";
- Data-security practices "exceed industry standards" or "surpass industry security standards";
- Consumer information is "stored in a bank-level hosting and security environment";

- Dwolla encrypts data "utilizing the same standards required by the federal government".

Some of these claims sound like "puffing" or "sales-speak", but the CFPB took the statements literally and held Dwolla to its own standards. Talk about digging your own hole! Now ask yourselves, whether any of these claims look familiar? Do you or any of your payment vendors make the same claims? What have you done to verify whether these claims are accurate?

The Bureau alleged that the company failed in a number of areas, such as having data-security policies and procedures reasonable for its size and complexity; use appropriate measures to identify reasonably foreseeable security risks; have adequate training for employees that had access to consumer information; use encryption technologies to properly safeguard sensitive consumer information; practice secure software development with an affiliated website; data security training was not provided to its affiliated software developer; failure to monitor whether the software developer complied with the security practices Dwolla had implemented to govern software development operations; and failure to conduct risk assessments or penetration tests on part of its infrastructure.

As a result of its investigation, Dwolla agreed to the following in its Consent Decree:

- Establish a written, comprehensive data security plan;
- Implement data security policies and procedures;
- Designate a qualified person to coordinate and be accountable for the data-security program;

- Conduct data-security risk assessments twice a year;
- Conduct regular, mandatory employee training;
- Implement reasonable procedures for the selection and retention of service providers capable of maintaining security practices;
- Obtain an annual data-security audit from a qualified, independent third party; and
- $ 100,000. Fine.

It would be a mistake for dealers to read about this action and think that this matter isn't applicable to their business since they aren't a payments company. The mere fact that the CFPB took this action highlights the emphasis it places on this subject. Further, Director Cordray has stated that consent orders are detailed guidance for the industry, and that companies who do not heed their lessons are committing "compliance malpractice". The smart company will take a look at the terms of the consent decree and use it as a checklist to conduct a self-examination of its own practices.

The vast majority of BHPH dealers as well as finance companies and other lenders use third party payment platforms to enable the acceptance of electronic payments, payments over the internet, and various other channels. Companies should keep in mind the CFPB's previous guidance about dealing with third party vendors and the importance it has placed on due diligence in the selection process and ongoing audit and documentation. These vendors are subject to the same level of scrutiny as if it were the dealers' own. Likewise, be mindful of your own statements on websites, in marketing materials and other customer communications and verify accuracy when using words such as "encryption", "PCI compliant", "your information is safe", "state of the art security", and similar terms.

The Federal Trade Commission (FTC) has already been active in this area and in a Consent Order against Wyndham hotels it set forth requirements for a data security program that are similar to what's found in the Dwolla decree. It even published a booklet, Start with Security: Business Guide, which sets forth the lessons learned from various FTC cases and is a "must read" for businesses. It can be accessed on the FTC's website at FTC.gov. I highly recommend reading the entire booklet and then subjecting both yourself and applicable vendors to its standards. The following list, while not as extensive as the booklet, provides an overview of the points it raises:

1. Don't collect or use Personally identifiable information if you don't need to and keep it only as long as needed;
2. Have access controls to sensitive data;
3. Use secure passwords and authentication;
4. Store sensitive personally identifiable information securely and protect it during transmission;
5. Use firewalls and monitor network activity;
6. Secure remote access to the network;
7. Create policies and procedures when developing new products and train engineers in secure coding;
8. Monitor service providers, have written security standards in contracts and verify compliance through audit;
9. Stay current on vulnerabilities and solutions;

10. Secure paper and devices that contain personally identifiable information internally and secure disposal of them.

Finally, always be aware that both your business and the industry are changing, so it's important to have a plan in place to deal with changes that will come in the form of new rules, legal interpretations and regulatory guidance. Have someone that's ultimately responsible for data security and make sure they have the tools needed to succeed. Dealers should realize that the public has been bombarded with news stories of data breaches and many have been victims of identity theft. That means that they are familiar with the issue and place a value on a company being able to demonstrate its best practices.

CHAPTER SIX

Is Compliance Kicking Your A$$?

Lot's of folks struggle with implementing compliance initiatives. Sometimes it's a lack of subject matter expertise, other times it's a lack of bandwidth, and yes, I've seen instances where it's because the power's that be don't think it's important. What follows are some of my favorite articles on the general subject of how to effectively achieve the elusive "culture of compliance" at your business.

IS COMPLIANCE KICKING YOUR A$$?

Did the title of this article get your attention? I suppose it's a bit aggressive, but let's get real, for a large portion of this audience the answer is a resounding "YES". I can list a bunch of explanations for this unfortunate state of affairs: the explosion of state and federal regulation over the past 25 years; state regulators figuring out that levying fines against dealers can produce a healthy income stream; the CFPB expecting business of all sizes to comply with the mandates of consent decrees it enters into with some of the industry's largest participants; the media; Plaintiff's lawyers; the internet. They all contribute to varying degrees. Who cares? It doesn't really matter how we got here, the fact is we're here, and a good many of you get your compliance %!* kicked on a regular basis.

Why? For starters, this article will be published in late January or early February, meaning it's right in the middle of perhaps the most sacred annual event in our industry: Tax Season. I'm being somewhat facetious, but then again I'm not, because after guiding folks through the legal and compliance maze for over 20 years, I'm convinced that owners and other leaders aren't willing to initiate change in their business during tax season, especially when it relates to something like compliance, which is both complex and doesn't generate revenue. That means a quarter of the year is gone before they'll even consider changing their compliance process. By then, the mind-frame of "If it Ain't Broke - Don't Fix It" takes over and compliance initiatives get placed on the back burner behind business priorities. The result is that the same compliance problems continue and don't really change. There's only one problem with this cycle……IT IS BROKEN!!!!

I hate to hit our fine readers over the head or on the %!* with the reality stick, but lots of folks are falling far short when it comes to their compliance function. Too many of you either think you're too small a target, it will never happen to you, or that you can buy your way into compliance through software, policies and procedures or whatever other magic potion of the month is being thrust upon the industry. Save your money, because if you truly want to develop the fabled "Culture of Compliance", you've got to COMMIT to building your COMPLIANCE INFRASTRUCTURE, and that's a lot more work than simply buying a product or service.

Strong compliance starts at the top. It's my observation that the dealers with the most successful implementation of compliance initiatives have owners and other senior leaders willing to live and breathe compliance on a daily basis. They talk about its importance in meetings, take corrective action immediately when they see or hear something done incorrectly, send company-wide emails with reminders, and emphasize it in personnel development plans. They don't wait for a customer complaint or letter from a Plaintiff's attorney to take action, they have a plan in place and measure progress on a regular basis.

I saw a good example recently that I'll use to illustrate this point. A client attended one of the industry conferences last spring and participated in several of the compliance classes. He returned home with some great education materials. Being a leader that understands the critical importance of compliance, he didn't put them on the shelf, never again to see the light of day. Instead, he used those materials to train his staff and then he had each employee sign a sheet of paper that acknowledged receiving this training. Sure it took a bit of work, but think of how he stretched the value of the money he spent to attend the conference. Not only has he disseminated that knowledge so that his employees can do their jobs better, but he can demonstrate his compliance efforts if he needs to do so.

Contrast this mind set with the many dealers that make the common mistake of trying to "buy" their way into compliance through policies that never get implemented and certainly never get rolled out to employees through training. Similarly, many dealers are guilty of hiring a "Compliance Officer" in name but don't offer anything in the way of training or resources to bring about success. These "officers" are usually high achievers and loyal employees from other parts of the business that quickly fall prey to the "Peter Principal" because they have no background in compliance. In Texas, we call that "giving them the badge but not the gun". The results are often underwhelming, to put it kindly. For those reading this and shifting uncomfortably in your seats, ask yourselves this question: Are you comfortable with your Compliance Officer dealing directly with a state or federal regulator on an audit or other complex matter?

It's time to confront the brutal fact that the need for a foundation and structure of compliance is real and isn't going away. The rules of our business have changed and your businesses are at risk if you don't change with the times. Plenty of folks try to buy compliance and hope that they can stay one step ahead of the hangman. It's time to give your compliance function the same commitment, resources and attention as the parts of the business that generate revenue, and acknowledge that falling short in this area can cost you that revenue you've worked so hard to create.

For those serious about taking the next step in their compliance evolution, reach out to me at the email address below, contact me on our website, or follow me on Twitter and I'll share thoughts on where to go from here. For those that don't share this commitment, I wish you much success in 2017.

MAKE COMPLIANCE AS BASIC AS PUTTING ON YOUR SOCKS

I grew up watching lots of basketball and had an obsession with John Wooden's UCLA Bruins. Coach Wooden's pyramid of success and team-building philosophies were later adopted by lots of businesses and he enjoyed a second career as a motivational speaker and author of numerous books. His pearls of wisdom such as "Failing to Prepare is Preparing to Fail", "If You Don't Have time to do it Right, When Will you have Time to Do it Over?" and It's the Little Details that are Vital. Little things make Big Things Happen" can be found in corporate communications and gyms alike.

The First Day of Practice

One of my favorite stories about this legendary coach is that on the first day of practice every season, he'd assemble his team and demonstrate the right way to put on socks and sneakers. His logic was that if his players had blisters they would not be able to play effectively. Therefore, he made them re-learn this basic skill they'd been doing almost their entire lives. Some of these players thought this lesson was quaint and outdated; however, many of them later brought their kids to Coach Wooden so he could teach them this same lesson.

This anecdote came to me earlier this spring while I was in the midst of attending industry conferences and observed the sheer flood of compliance information that is being thrust upon our industry. An array of speakers, so-called experts, and compliance vendors have come out of the woodwork like prospectors during the gold rush. The audience is bombarded with a litany of calls to action to manage risk and build a compliance mindset but is given little practical guidance on how this should be done. They end up buying tools like software, templates and kits that provide a false sense of security but that end up under-utilized because there is not a simple way to implement.

Let's Get Back to the Basics

How do we get back to the basics? How should we put on our socks and sneakers? FIRST, it is imperative to have a POLICY AND PROCEDURE MANUAL to set forth both the operational expectations and the overall emphasis that each employee is responsible to know and follow the law. This goal sounds a lot simpler than it is because dealers can slip up on their compliance when they get too focused on their operational needs at the expense of their legal ones. To resolve this potential conflict, I recommend that the managers over the various departments set forth the key components of their strategies and practices. Then the policy and procedure manual can be built around the actual business practices and scaled accordingly.

I personally prefer a policy manual that is short, sweet and to the point. My logic is that a smaller manual is easier for employees to understand and follow, plus, in the event of litigation, it won't be so cumbersome as to trip up employees.

To summarize on this first point, the policies and procedures manual is your "get out of jail cheaper, if not free card" in the event of a legal challenge because you will be able to demonstrate that your stated company goal was to be compliant and follow the law and that any deviation from that goal was unintentional and a mistake. The problem can be limited to the failings of one employee in a particular instance rather than indicate a widespread company failing.

My SECOND key to compliance is TRAINING. In my experience, this is the area where companies fall short. You can have the best policies and procedures manual in the world, but it won't do you a lick of good if it's sitting in someone's desk and has never been "rolled out" to the folks doing the actual work. Companies may have good intentions and spend the time and money to develop a great manual, but then daily events, month end goals, and employee attrition get in the way and pretty soon there is a climate where the policy manual is a fictitious aspiration rather than daily reality.

Instead, keep a written training calendar to serve as a record of when every employee receives training. In my humble opinion, no employee should go no more than a few months without some form of training and reinforcement. As a practical matter, a lot of training happens "one on one", so it's up to managers and supervisors to follow up and put a notation in the personnel file to indicate that training was received. Even better, have the employee sign or initial such page to indicate that training was received. "If it isn't written down it didn't happen" is the approach that must be taken because you can be sure that a plaintiff's lawyers will make that argument.

Challenge your supervisors to develop training materials. One large client built its training into its monthly performance review meeting. You'd better believe that prioritized the issue in the minds of the employees. Similarly, a small car lot with only a few employees chose to call attention to training by having a monthly brown bag lunch in which a different training topic was presented, either by me or by an employee chosen to present the material. The effect this had on the knowledge of the staff was tremendous.

THIRDLY, take advantage of PROGRESSIVE DISCIPLINE, which requires documenting bad behavior on an escalating basis. Again, in my experience most companies, big and small alike, fall short here. Don't just correct a credit underwriter that strays from policy or a collector that does something wrong, but make a note of such a verbal warning and put it in the employee's personnel file. If it happens again make it a written warning. If it keeps happening then take appropriate action for the given situation. Demonstrating the serious nature of compliance to your employees will also allow you to demonstrate your commitment to plaintiff's lawyers, regulators and even your own capital providers and other third party relationships.

FINALLY, take a hard look at HOW YOU HANDLE CUSTOMER COMPLAINTS and build a complaint management system that's in line with the complexity of your business. Thirty years ago a list of complaints on a legal pad may have done the trick. Fifteen years ago that list would have been kept on a sortable excel spreadsheet. Now, software allows us to track these complaints and look for commonality and trends. The key is to teach your employees what is and isn't a complaint, how to record and categorize them, teaching what constitutes effective and timely response, and ultimately resolve the complaint and create a satisfied customer. All of this information should be tracked across the company so that larger issues can be identified. Most importantly, the business should be able to instantly supply the list and demonstrate its commitment to resolution.

Conclusions

So there you have it, the compliance lawyer's equivalent of putting on socks and sneakers. Now I encourage everyone to share this across their business and honestly evaluate where there are opportunities for improvement. In the words of Coach Wooden…"Failure is not fatal, but failure to change might be".

TIME FOR YOUR COMPLIANCE CHECK-UP

With a New Year upon us, it's a good time for dealers to do what the rest of us do, schedule their annual check-up. Don't worry, there are no needles involved and it won't be too invasive, because the focus is limited to your dealership's compliance. Okay, so on second thought it may not be so pleasant.

Assessing current compliance efforts will go a long way towards building the foundation of success for the year. To get started, much like the check-up you get at the doctor's office, I'm going to ask a series of questions, and the answers will help determine the vitality of your compliance related health.

Who is in Charge?

First, is there anyone actually in-charge and accountable for compliance, or do you leave it up to everyone to "do their share"? In my experience, a common trait among dealers that make a weak effort at compliance is that they fail to put someone in charge. In order to avoid that mistake, appoint a compliance officer. It must be communicated to everyone in the organization that this person has authority and the support of management and the owner(s). Next, the compliance officer should be given training and resources so that they can become an expert. There are a wide variety of tools out there and the cost doesn't have to be crippling, so find what's right for the size and complexity of your business. Having someone in charge of this important function will go a long way towards success.

What are the Biggest Concerns?

Secondly, ask your chief compliance officer, or some of your leaders if you've yet to appoint one, about their biggest concerns from a compliance and risk perspective. Are there products or services offered that cause discomfort? Has there been a drastic change in your key business metrics, either up or down? Are there third party service providers whose practices keep folks up at night? Has there been an increase in customer complaints, lawsuits or regulator inquiries? All of these things can be indicators of compliance issues buried beneath the surface. Once the list is made don't just set it aside, make it a goal to give each of the items attention and investigate why concerns have been raised and take action.

Do you have Written Policies?

Having written policies sounds simple enough, but a lot of dealers don't know where to begin so they just never get around to it. Start with the basics: on the front end of the business there should be an underwriting policy, credit reporting/equal credit opportunity act policy and policies related to things like OFAC and Red Flags. That's not a comprehensive list but it's a good place to start. On the back end of the business, there should be a Servicing and Collections Policy and one to guide the handling of customer complaints. Again, that's not a complete list but it gets the wheels turning. Next, consider having policies governing your employees' use of technology because there is a lot of risk in this area. Again, the needs of any specific dealer will vary based on the size and complexity of the business involved. The bottom line, though, is that written policies will provide consistency and a framework on which to build.

Is Training Provided to Employees?

Written policies will do no good, though, if they're simply sitting on a desk. The key to having policies is to get employees to use them and that's where training comes in. The best operators I've seen take training of personnel seriously and view it as an investment in their business. They teach them the expectations for their position as well as comprehensive company values. Operators that aren't as successful tend to look at training as an expense and a distraction. Which are you?

Training takes a lot of different forms and, again, a lot of it is based on the size and complexity of the business. A large company with dozens of employees spread out over a handful of locations might utilize online training to assure consistency, while a single location dealership may do a lot of hands-on training where the owner works directly with personnel. There is no "right" formula. The question to ask is whether the dealership is giving each employee **all** of the information necessary to do their job effectively. I emphasize "all" because very often folks take a narrow view. For instance, it's just as important for a collector to learn relevant debt collection laws as it is to learn how to use the phone system and account management software.

Is there a Complaint Management Process?

Having a process for handling customer complaints is important from both a risk perspective and because it's just plain good business. Do your employees know what to do when they receive a complaint? Do they all even have the same understanding of what constitutes a complaint? If a complaint is received, are your personnel empowered to try to fix the problem or do complaints fall through the cracks because of a lack of understanding on how to proceed? Finally, are complaints tracked and analyzed so that management can identify trends and common problems, such as whether complaints involve individual employees or a particular product or service offered to customers? Being able to answer all of these questions in the affirmative will allow for better customer service, retention and an overall experience.

Is there a Culture of Compliance?

This question has to do with whether the subject of compliance receives emphasis on a regular basis or is it "out of sight out of mind"? Compliance should be inter-woven with business systems and processes, like my example of the collector learning about relevant debt collection laws in addition to how to use the tools provided to do the job. Employees should know the compliance risks associated with their job duties and what resources are available. They should also know that they are accountable for compliant behavior. One of the best ways of making employees accountable is by using progressive discipline, whereby there is a documented system in place so that a company can demonstrate its expectations regarding performing duties in a compliant manner. By way of example, if an employee tasked with handling customer complaints instead ignored a complaint that was later brought to the attention of management, the employee should receive some type of verbal or written warning which is then documented in the employees file, thus demonstrating the company's commitment to following its own policies and process and doing things right.

Are Industry Developments Considered?

This question simply asks whether management is aware or oblivious to the big picture. At a minimum, the folks that run a dealership should be aware of what actions their state regulator has recently taken against other dealers, what type of cases other dealers are being sued about, and what complaints are being filed either on the internet or with the Better Business Bureau. Are there subjects that your local or state industry association is focusing on? Is there familiarity with larger events such as when the Federal Trade Commission levies an advertising fine against a dealer or the Consumer Financial Protection Bureau fines a dealer such as in the Herbie's matter? Remember, the Director of the CFPB has stated that failure to follow such guidance is "compliance malpractice", so be proactive, learn from what's going on around you, and change business practices as situations require.

What Are Your Compliance Goals for the New Year?

Everybody reading this publication can probably name their key business goals on a yearly and even monthly basis in terms of how many vehicles they plan to move, growth rate for their portfolio, and key metrics such as "look to book" and "Repo Rate". I encourage you to do the same thing on the compliance side. I know success is more difficult to measure in this area because the subject itself is so nebulous, but establishing key compliance goals will allow you to define success. Whether it's establishing a new written policy every month, developing a regular training schedule or a formalized complaint management process, the key is to set the goal and then create the roadmap to achieve it. Compliance doesn't just happen, and the journey won't be quick, but by giving serious consideration to the questions raised in this article, you'll be on your way to significantly upgrading your compliance capabilities.

YOU ARE WHAT YOUR RECORD SAYS YOU ARE

As I write this I'm sitting in my hastily put together home office, the result of the Coronavirus outbreak. Like a lot of you, I'm now dealing with simple issues like connectivity and more difficult ones like how to keep the business running and help our clients. I hope things are somewhat more back to normal by the time you read this. Maybe they will be, maybe they won't be, my hunch is it will be somewhere in between. What I do know though is that life will go on, business will go on in some form or fashion, so in writing this article I thought I'd share something relevant which I've observed over the past few weeks.

What's Bill Parcells Got to do with a Pandemic?

The title of this article, " You are what your record says you are", is one of my favorite quotes from football coach Bill Parcells. As great a coach as he was, and he has the wins and titles to prove it, he was perhaps even a better source of practicality and wisdom, and always a fertile ground of memorable one liners for the reporters that covered him. This quote was his response to those coaches, owners and even fans that "reason away" their disappointing record with excuses like "we had too many injuries", "we had bad breaks this year", and "if the ball had just bounced another way a few times". He was essentially saying "nonsense", over the course of a season those things balance out and the record at the end is the correct measure of where things stand with the team.

So what's all of this got to do with a pandemic and our current crisis? Although we're only a short time in, I have already begun to see that the Coach's quote is an accurate analogy for business. Quite frankly, some of you were prepared to handle a crisis and some weren't, and the common denominator, as far as I've been able to tell from my limited sample size of clients that I work with regularly, is strong leadership and a plan.

Whether dealing with a health crisis, natural disaster, or some other emergency, strong leaders have already assembled a team to perform when the going gets tough. They anticipate that bad things will happen at some point and have a culture that is ready to rise to the challenge. For example, this crisis has created challenges in staffing and personnel. Those that had a resource with a strong human resources background and an Employee Handbook already in effect were able to deal with those issues better than those that didn't and didn't have a map to follow.

Similarly, some of you have strong collection policies and procedures and have trained staff and have the rules ingrained in their daily performance. They've already got a plan in place to handle critical issues that arise in a crisis like deferments, they've got a strategy to address customer questions and concerns, and haven't had to hit the panic button and make things up as they go along and hope that they aren't creating liability for a later day.

I was so proud over the weekend when I saw a client's Facebook Page post to their customers that communicated how its dealership was responding to the crisis. They covered what they are doing to keep the facility safe for employees and the general public, the best ways for customers to make payments and communicate with them, and their plan for the next few weeks, both if they remain open and in the event they are forced to close. Internally, this dealership communicated with all employees on the current status of things and what the plan is for company wide communication going forward. That's proactive leadership, and it's critical in difficult times.

I look at my job as helping you protect your businesses from risk, whether it's compliance risk, regulatory dangers, lawsuits, etc. I'm fortunate to deal with people that are talking to me because the issue is important to them. Some are proactive and seek us out before they "need" us, while others only find religion after a storm hits. In either case, once we start working together we can do a lot of good. My message to you is "do the work". If you are doing some good things to protect your business already, do some more, if you haven't been devoted to this in the past then now is the time to start.

My challenge/invitation to everyone is to weather this storm as best you can, stay healthy, and get prepared for the good things that are ahead of us. They will come! So make sure you are in the best position to enjoy those blessings when they come your way.

CRISIS MANAGEMENT STARTS WITH LEADERSHIP AND PLANNING

As I write this I'm sitting in my hastily put together home office, the result of the Coronavirus outbreak. Like a lot of you, I'm now dealing with simple issues like connectivity and more difficult ones like how to keep the business running and help our clients. There is a lot of fear and uncertainty, and even though this crisis is in its early stages, I've already had some difficult conversations with clients about personnel and business operations. To be candid, a lot of folks had never taken any steps to prepare for a crisis.

Crisis management is something that's unpleasant but has to be done. When I first started writing for this publication I was General Counsel for AutoStar Solutions, a DMS provider. One of my best contributions there was implementing a monthly threat assessment exercise. I'd gather Allen Dobbins, the CEO, and some other key business leaders and present a hypothetical crisis situation. I would develop made up facts on my own and not share them with anyone beforehand.

One month the scenario presented was our experiencing a hacking event, the next it was a natural disaster like a tornado wiping out our office. I remember one time I hypothesized our receiving bad publicity across the industry due to a client being investigated by a regulator, and another involved a mass exodus of clients. After I presented the scenario, we'd sit for a few hours and discuss our response plan among the various departments and business functions, taking extensive notes. Then we'd develop an action plan and put it in a drawer, hopefully never to be used. We rotated some of the key personnel over time so that even mid-level managers got exposure to the planning sessions and they provided valuable insight into our response efforts.

I've been thinking a lot about those meetings during the past few days as this crisis has unfolded. We were always busy and pressed for time, so it would have been easy to cancel these meetings for urgent business issues, but I never remember a month where we moved the threat assessment exercise. That's because Allen Dobbins was a strong leader and he knew that preparedness for tough times was critical to business survival.

Whether dealing with a health crisis, natural disaster, or some other emergency, strong leaders like Allen think ahead and develop a plan for tough times. They anticipate that bad things will happen at some point and have a culture that is ready to rise to the challenge. For example, our current crisis has created challenges in staffing and personnel. Those clients that already have a resource with a strong human resources background and a Employee Handbook already in effect have been able to deal with those issues better than those that didn't have a map to follow.

Similarly, some of you have strong collection policies and procedures and have trained staff and have the rules ingrained in their daily performance. There is already a plan in place to handle critical issues that arise in a crisis like deferments and a strategy to address widespread customer emergencies. The ones that prepared didn't have to hit the panic button and make things up as they go along and hope that they aren't creating liability for a later day.

In the first days of the crisis we were inundated with calls from clients. We thought the best way to help them was to take advantage of the shared knowledge we all have, so we hosted several phone conferences and webinars for folks to have the opportunity to learn from each other. Collectively, we addressed HR and personnel issues, customer challenges, and the unique challenges of selling vehicles and collecting accounts in the midst of a pandemic. We had dealer principals participate along with account managers, clerks and managers. Thanks go out to those that participated, that's proactive leadership, and it's critical in difficult times.

At Ignite, we look at our jobs as helping you protect your businesses from risk, whether its compliance risk, regulatory dangers, lawsuits, etc. I'm fortunate to deal with people that are talking to me because the issue is important to them. Some are proactive and seek us out before they "need" us, while others only find religion after a storm hits. In either case, once we start working together we can do a lot of good. My message to you is "do the work". If you are already doing some good things to protect your business, whether that's compliance work, threat assessments, or something else, keep doing it, and if you haven't been devoted to this in the past then now is the time to start.

Everyone must weather this storm as best you can and get prepared for the good things that are ahead of us. They will come! So develop a strong plan to help you through, lean on the knowledge of others, learn from each other, and make sure you are in the best position to enjoy those blessings when they come your way.

DON'T GET BURNED ON COMPLIANCE DURING THE LAZY DAYS OF SUMMER

In my experience, summer is a notoriously slow time for compliance initiatives. In between vacation schedules and July 4th sales, compliance is placed on the back burner. That's a mistake and a missed opportunity, because now is the perfect time to do a compliance "tune up" on some issues that tend to get swept under the rug once things get busier. Here are some ideas based on some repetitive issues we've seen over the past few months:

Website

A website review is one of the first things I do when taking on a new client. It gives me a window into the operations of the business through the eyes of the consumer and shows me the things the dealer thinks are important. Unfortunately, I tend to find some pretty significant issues that need attention.

It's important to note that websites are considered advertising in the eyes of the Federal Trade Commission ("FTC"), so all of those statements being made mean something and can be used against the dealer if found to be incorrect. Even more alarming is that the internet makes it extremely easy for your state or federal regulator to "let their fingers to the walking" and see your business practices with relative ease. Therefore, it's critical that dealers get their sites reviewed regularly by competent professionals, preferably before the content is live.

Some of the issues I've recently seen that cause my heart to flutter include:

"Internet special" prices on vehicles. Having different internet pricing can create legal liability;

Touting "certified" programs without supporting information. Also, the FTC views certified programs as a safety claim, so it expects to see information regarding recalls and provide the viewer with a link to check whether the vehicle is subject to a recall;

Use of some but not all trigger terms. Repeat after me……down payment, amount of finance charge, payment amount, term. If you provide one of these terms you need to provide all of them. Too often I see dealers call attention to only one term and omit the rest. That's just too easy for the regulators to jump on.

Online credit applications that leave out necessary language. Credit applications can create liability! Too often I see condensed versions that leave out critical language that protects the dealer. If your online credit application is much shorter than your paper one, I suggest you seek the advice of a professional. Also, if you are accepting online applications electronically there should be relevant language about security, safeguarding of information, and a robust submission process.

Terms for use of websites. Dealers can create issues by simply having a website. One way to curtail this potential liability is to have terms of use. Information regarding electronic disclosures and privacy and security are also topics that may be addressed.

Payment portals. The ability to accept payments online is a great tool to offer consumers. Unfortunately, many dealers are oblivious to the plethora of potential issues and think their third party service provider is covering all of the bases. They often are not, or if they are, their terms of use protect the third party but not the dealer. It's a good idea to have terms that directly protect the dealer.

Facebook and other Social Media

Dealers are using Facebook to sell a lot of cars. Unfortunately, everything I said about websites being advertising also applies to Facebook and other social media. It's important to teach this to personnel, because I've seen very few posts that withstand careful scrutiny. In fact, I recommend having a social media policy that sets forth the rules for these ads and who is authorized to post them. Having a professional craft a template that can be used repetitively is also a good idea.

I also like to see employment policy manuals that clearly give the dealership ownership of its content and a social media administrator that is responsible for all passwords. I know of one dealership that spent a significant sum of money on attorneys seeking an injunction against a disgruntled former employee that essentially locked the dealer out of its own page. Be proactive and address these issues up front in employment agreements.

Craigslist and other Social Media

I've heard lots of dealers speak favorably about the sales lift they get from their Craigslist "advertising", yet they scoff when I remind them that it truly is advertising and subject to those same pesky rules I mentioned above. This is especially true when failing to use all of the disclosures in the trigger term requirements. I've also noticed a tendency to use industry jargon or abbreviations that can create unintended consequences. What's even worse, I find that many sales people list vehicles on the site in such a way that could leave a consumer to believe the vehicle is sold by an individual and not a dealership. That fact pattern could easily be turned into a lawsuit of deceptive or even abusive practices. Again, there should be controls in place governing the content of these listings.

Vendor Management

There is a lot written on the subject of vendor management and I mention it again here because I think this is a great opportunity for a real world example of where "the rubber meets the road". Too often the dealer thinks that it is throwing any potential liability over the fence by hiring a third party service provider. Frequently, though, the contracts being signed leave all liability back with the vendor. I've seen examples of this with a print advertising vendor as well as a website provider.

The remedy is strong contracts and due diligence. Know who you are entering into business with and make sure they have the desired expertise. Make sure the contract clearly explains which party is responsible for certain behaviors and have the vendor represent and warrant its services. Vendor contracts are usually one sided. The good news is that they are also negotiable. The dealer can handle the business terms, but seek out the help of qualified professionals to craft a fair agreement.

Conclusions.

Think your compliance work is done for the summer? Think again! This article provides a great starting point of opportunities for improvement. These are often overlooked, especially during the busiest sales months, so now is a great time to take control of these areas and get your house in order for the rest of the year. As always, we're here to help if you have questions or would like more information.

DO YOUR METRICS SUPPORT YOUR OBSESSION WITH JUDICIAL REPOSSESSION?

As a young lawyer just starting my career, I cut my teeth representing used car dealers and finance companies in just about every type of dispute imaginable. Very often I was called upon to use the courts to recover vehicles that had proven impossible to repossess by the traditional means of the tow truck. In these cases, called sequestrations, replevins, or claim and delivery, depending on the jurisdiction, the creditor asks the court to order law enforcement (usually the sheriff) to recover its collateral.

I handled these matters with regularity and they produced some great stories, ranging from the sheriff that called me during an actual gunfight with a customer, to the sheriff that told me he was looking at the vehicle but couldn't repossess it because it was at the bottom of the customer's pool. Those are tales for another article, though, because the focus on this one concerns the efficient use of judicial repossessions and knowing when to pull the trigger.

The judicial recovery process can be quite expensive. There are filing fees with the court, the purchase of a bond (which most jurisdictions require the creditor to acquire to protect the defendant/owner in the event the collateral is wrongfully taken), service of process fees, and the attorney's fees, all of which are incurred whether or not the collateral recovery is successful, not to mention sheriff and tow truck fees if the vehicle is recovered. If a creditor isn't careful, it can end up chasing good money with bad with nothing to show for it.

In many of these early cases, the results were not worth the client's investment because the customer/defendant could not be served (the car can't just be picked up, the customer has to be served with the lawsuit) or because the value of the collateral wasn't worth the expense. Later, I developed a screening process to try to help clients boost the success rate of these cases. After all, I knew that a poor result for a client would ultimately hurt me in the long run.

The three cornerstones of my guidelines were: a) a good address to serve the defendant with the suit; b) reasonable certainty that the value of the collateral would be at least twice as much as the fees and costs that would be incurred; and c) no glaring deficiencies in the file that suggest that a counter-claim would be filed. These suggestions worked and the success rate for these cases, and my clients' recoveries went up significantly. These guidelines still work today, but in our work with dealers across the country, we often find that there is no strategy developed on when to use the judicial recovery process and personnel aren't trained on the nuances of such cases.

I've seen plenty of personnel make emotional decisions to pursue a judicial recovery when there were other factors that suggested not to go in that direction. Sometimes the way companies track their accounts provides an incentive to take a difficult account and move it to "legal" status. I've seen instances where personnel think about that week or month's metrics and don't consider the overall cost that the company will incur.

That's why it's important to understand both "hard" and "soft" costs associated with judicial recovery: How much time does it take personnel to track and handle these cases? What kind of billing arrangement is agreed to with legal counsel? What hard costs like filing, sheriff and bond fees are going to be incurred? Finally, are there risk factors not being considered? I'm specifically referring to those kinds of allegations that give rise to counter-claims. This is a crucial issue that requires objective analysis, because if a counterclaim is filed the creditor can be stuck in the case indefinitely and spend much more money than it intended.

Conclusions:

Judicial recovery of collateral can be a valuable tool to help creditors, but an objective analysis of the expense and the likelihood of recovery should be conducted prior to involving an attorney and the courts. Analyze your results of past cases to provide some meaningful benchmarks on how to proceed in the future. We'll be glad to talk you through some of the issues and help develop a meaningful strategy.

THE DETAILS ARE EVERYTHING

"THE DETAILS ARE EVERYTHING!" A former law school professor used to bellow that phrase to our class on a regular basis. A few years later, as a young lawyer, I heard this phrase again while being admonished by a senior partner as I was preparing for a cross examination of a witness. It turns out these nuggets of wisdom stayed with me over the years, as I was reminded of this phrase and its lessons a few times in the past month in various client issues that arose.

The Matter of the Extended Service Contract

In the first matter, a BHPH dealer client sent me a demand letter it had received regarding the extended service contract it sold. The crux of the customer's argument was that the extended service contract said in black and white that only vehicles with less than 100,000 miles were eligible, but the vehicle in question had 150,000 miles at the time of sale. THE DETAILS ARE EVERYTHING! My client's position was that it and the provider would honor the terms of the service contract anyway and that it had made an innocent mistake, but the attorney for the customer was demanding that the entire transaction be unwound because of the amount financed being inflated by the service contract, imputing all sorts of deceptive and nefarious practices on my client and threatening a lawsuit. My client wisely opted to resolve the issue rather than incur the defense costs, and then revised its various documents and trained its team on what the documents said to make sure the house was in order in the future.

Is it a GPS Device or Theft Deterrent?

Next, a new client reached out because a customer was complaining that she was misled about the GPS device that had been installed in her vehicle as a condition of financing. While the dealer did disclose the existence of the device in a letter that it has each customer sign upon contracting, it was described as a "theft deterrent device" that would "be used to locate the location of the vehicle upon theft". The problem arose when the customer was late on payments and the client's personnel allegedly told the customer that the vehicle's location was being observed and they knew where it was parked and would repossess it if payment wasn't made.

I'll leave the training opportunity lecture for another day, but this consumer's argument was focused on the fact that the letter she signed only discussed use in the event of theft, it didn't say anything about using the device to verify location upon default, nor did it address privacy considerations. Once again, THE DETAILS ARE EVERYTHING!, and it's much better to resolve a complaint such as this when an angry customer is threatening to call the state regulator and post to social media.

Credit Dispute Letters in Disguise

Finally, there's the recent example of various credit dispute form letters that are making their way from one company to the next. I don't think a week goes by without one of our clients calling and looking for guidance. There are several variations of the letter, but they all seem to start off with alleging a Fair Debt Collection Practices Act ("FDCPA") violation because the recipient is a third party debt collector. Of course, the vast majority of our clients are first party collectors because they collect their own accounts, and the FDCPA reference is mis-applied. Several companies that choose to reply to these letters point out this fact, while a great many folks just end up tossing the letters aside and don't even respond.

However, THE DETAILS ARE EVERYTHING!, and somewhere in these letters, usually buried after paragraphs of legal bloviating, is a single sentence that asserts a credit dispute based on what information is being reported to the credit reporting agencies. The problem is, most folks never bother to read the entire letter because they never get past the FDCPA allegation. In fact, I'm convinced that these letters are intentionally designed to encourage this, giving rise to allegations of violations of the Fair Credit Reporting Act ("FCRA") for failure to respond to the dispute in accordance with the statute. Lawsuits based on FCRA allegations are still the most commonly asserted against creditors.

Embrace the Details

In each of these instances, the details came back to bite the dealer. So what's the best way to protect your businesses? EMBRACE THE DETAILS! Get a thorough document review that will identify issues like the ones presented in the first two examples. Review your process for functions like complaint handling and review of dispute letters and train your team sufficiently so that they are aware of the importance of the details. Set up some routine audit items so that the business has confidence in the quality of its account servicing. We all know that there are a slew of regulations and laws that require attention, so be proactive and address these types of items before they come back to haunt you. Good luck, and as always, feel free to reach out to share your own experiences or ask questions.

SOMETIMES SIMPLE ADVICE IS BEST

At Ignite's recently concluded Compliance Unleashed Conference, we were fortunate to have my friend Jessica Lesser deliver the keynote speech. Jessica is a consumer finance attorney that currently practices with the law firm of Maurice & Wutscher where she defends creditors in all sorts of lawsuits. We selected Jessica to deliver this address because of her diverse and unique background. In her nearly 30 year career, in addition to her current role, she's been in-house counsel at AmeriCredit, served as the head of consumer protection at the Dallas Office of the Texas Attorney General, and had her own plaintiff's firm where she sued creditors. With that kind of background, we were pretty confident that her presentation wouldn't be "run of the mill", and we sure were correct!

Her advice to our audience was simple and brilliant, with some Texas bluntness thrown in. She summed up her many experiences by passing on two pillars of wisdom that she stresses to her clients: "Show you Care" and "Own Your Stuff" (I've made a slight deviation to that last word out of respect for our more modest readers). With about three decades of experience in this field under my belt, I found myself nodding in fervent agreement, so let's go into these concepts a bit deeper.

Show You Care

This sounds like such simple guidance, yet so many struggle with it. Like Jessica, I'm always preaching to my clients that their company culture has to include some empathy for its customers. Not all customer complaints are an attempt to avoid responsibility. Sometimes a company's actions can fall short or there can be a confluence of unfortunate circumstances. It's the responsibility of the company to teach its personnel how to listen to its customers and evaluate events that have transpired. To me, demonstrating a concern for its own actions is a great way to "show you care", and it all starts with complaint management.

I often find that even well intentioned companies struggle with the complaint management function. It requires a strong process, "buy in" throughout the company, and a willingness to listen to the customer's perspective with an open mind. Why is this so important? Well, for starters, in my experience, almost every lawsuit I ever defended started out as a complaint that wasn't resolved in a satisfactory manner. Secondly, unresolved complaints tend to percolate up to and get the attention of regulators, and that can make a company find religion real fast.

I am of the belief that if a company provides the customer with a pathway to complain and shows a willingness to work through the issue, the customer will have a more favorable view of the company, even if the process didn't result in the customer getting exactly what they wanted. What are some basic ways to demonstrate you care? For starters, I tell my clients to put "tell us how we are doing" signage around their stores along with an email address or phone number dedicated to handling customer matters, as well as having a prominent banner on its website with the same information. That's just a start though, because then there has to be a team trained on monitoring and resolving those matters that come in.

Next, invite customer feedback during "welcome" calls and in similar letters. Again, just by showing an interest in the customer's experience, you're going a long way to diffusing potential negative situations. Finally, teach personnel the importance of listening and not "talking at" the customer. This simple tool can de-escalate an adverse situation by showing a willingness to tackle a problem together.

Own Your Stuff

When Jessica challenged the audience with this statement, I could feel the energy in the Conference hall increase, as folks sat up straighter in their seats and gave her their undivided attention. The message was clear: Accept your share of responsibility.

I've been involved in a lot of cases where my clients did just the opposite, they tried to deflect attention onto the customer's behavior or the failings of some other third party, never willing to take a hard look in the mirror and examine their role. For instance, I had a client stubbornly cling to the "I sold the car As -Is" argument in a case where the engine seized within a week, unwilling to consider the risk and cost in defending the customer's case, which was built around implied warranties of merchantability and fitness for a particular purpose claims, and well as more nebulous (and dangerous) state deceptive acts and practices laws that included even broader wording. Needless to say, that case didn't end well.

In another matter, I was defending a company that had some let's just say "overly aggressive" collectors. My client's focus was solely directed at the customer's failure to pay on time and its resulting breach under the contract, while ignoring that this was a sympathetic customer who had previously paid on time and who then didn't make payments due to a medical emergency. The consumer's attorney, on the other hand, was focused on the fact that my client's staff hadn't received any kind of training on federal and state collection laws. Again, the client's mistake was looking outward, at the actions of the customer, rather than reflecting on what it could have done better.

So what does "own your stuff" mean to me? It means honestly evaluating the facts of a matter objectively and being willing to consider mistakes that may have been made. It means being a critical thinker rather than an emotional one, and it is a call to confront unfavorable facts with an eye towards fixing the problem and not the blame. Make this a part of your company culture and you've gone a long way towards a better customer experience and a better company.

Conclusions

I want to thank Jessica Lesser for these pearls of wisdom that she passed on to our audience. Although I don't have her background in either representation of plaintiffs or as a regulator, I think it's pretty telling that we both have the same point of view when it comes to defending creditors. So "show you care" and "own your stuff"! You'll be grateful that you did.

COMPLIANCE MOVES TO MAKE IN 2022

As we bring 2021 to a close, I want to encourage this audience to reflect: How much progress did you make in Compliance and protecting your business this year? I know everyone (well almost everyone) starts with the best of intentions, but then life and business happen and matters that aren't urgent continually get pushed down on the list. By the time you look up, year end is right around the corner and not much progress has been made. Think about my question again. Can you point to specific progress that you've made?

Whatever your answer, I'm confident that next year you'll be able to recite a list of accomplishments because in this article I'm going to share with you compliance moves that will protect your business and make you feel great about your progress in 2022. Am I giving away the "keys to the kingdom"? Yes, but it's the holiday season.

January is the month to set goals

Let's get the year kicked off right. Management should meet with the person ultimately responsible for company compliance and set some goals for the year. What, you don't have such a person? Appoint one now, and then get them some training on what's involved in being in charge of compliance.

Challenge your compliance resource to develop meaningful metrics based on compliance related indicators so that regular reporting can occur (if you need help identifying those just ask me). Schedule quarterly compliance meetings where developments will be discussed and issues identified. Get the year started by committing to good habits and regular communication about compliance topics.

Speaking of good habits, my company Ignite Consulting Partners offers a free monthly webinar series, usually held the third Tuesday of each month at 2:00 CST. These are coordinated sessions throughout the year that present strategic ideas as well as covering timely issues and attendees get a Certificate of Attendance. Participating in this series is a great way to achieve demonstrable compliance training for your organization. We record the sessions so you don't have to attend live. Email us at info@IgniteCP.com if you'd like more information on how to register.

February is the month to review Policy content

It's been my observation that at one time or another lot's of folks "find religion" and decide to create written compliance policies to govern operations like collections, sales, and underwriting and important compliance topics like complaint management, credit furnishing and dispute handling, and information security. Unfortunately, it's also my observation that a lot of folks stop there and don't use their policies to serve as guardrails for their business. Not in 2022! Let's blow the dust off of your Compliance Management System and those policies and make sure they are current and up to date. Revise sections that no longer accurately reflect your business, and create new ones where needed. Please reach out if you want to discuss the key policies that I think every independent dealer should have.

March into a Document Review

I'm a huge believer that at least once a year a dealer should get a thorough document review of every piece of paper (or screen for you e-contracting folks) a customer sees at closing. I do lots of deal jacket reviews, and I often find contradictory documents, wrong or incomplete information, and a myriad of other issues. Don't rely on your DMS or other forms provider to keep you safe. At least once a year you should have a qualified attorney or compliance professional review your deal jackets and provide a summary of findings.

Similarly, get a review of your website, collection and servicing letters, and advertising. Don't assume that your content always stays the same. I've seen important letters fall out of circulation and key words suddenly go missing from a letter. Spring is the time of renewal, so make sure your content is providing the intended protection.

April - Check out BHPH United's Inaugural Summit

Ignite Consulting Partners, has joined up with six other leading industry service providers to create BHPH United, which is dedicated to providing current, relevant and accurate education to BHPH dealers. As industry participants operating across the entire spectrum of the industry, our diverse expertise makes us uniquely positioned to achieve our goal to provide real world, practical and usable knowledge. Our inaugural Summit will be held at the Bellagio Resort & Casino on Sunday April 10, 2022 through Tuesday April 12, 2022. We will kick things off with a Welcome Gala on Sunday night followed up with two full days of interactive education and training from dealers and industry experts. Make plans to attend. Go to BHPHUnited.com for more information.

May - Make Plans to Attend Compliance Unleashed

If you want impactful compliance training, make plans to attend Ignite's 4th annual Compliance Unleashed Conference. It will be held May 16-18th in Dallas-Fort Worth. There is no other auto finance compliance education like this. We are solely focused on compliance training for the BHPH and independent dealers. Whether you are an owner, manager or compliance person, this is the conference that will teach you how to weave "best in class" practices into your operation and protect your business. We offer a day and a half of classes from some of the best speakers in the industry, and on Wednesday morning on the 18th we host an interactive workshop that will teach how to conduct self audits on key points in the business. This class alone can transform your business andl save thousands of dollars.

June's Focus is on Complaint Management

If you are a regular reader, or if you've heard me present on the importance of complaint management at a Conference, you've probably heard me say "every lawsuit I ever defended started out as a customer complaint that wasn't resolved". Strong complaint management is the best way to keep small problems from becoming big ones. Also, I can't tell you how many times I've seen regulator investigations start as consumer complaints.

What goes into strong complaint management? First, define what a complaint is, and make sure everyone in your company understands the definition. Next, figure out how complaints will be tracked. Will they be added to a spreadsheet, included in software, or someplace else? Don't just add them in notes to your DMS, you need to keep track of them separately so you can look at them in one concise place. Who will be responsible for entering this information? Will they funnel through one person, or are various personnel in different departments all responsible for entering the information? Who is responsible for resolving complaints and making decisions on whether there is any relief to the customer? Finally, develop a habit of looking at your complaints on a monthly and quarterly basis, and look to see whether there are repetitive complaints that suggest an opportunity to improve your business.

July and August are the Times to Attend State Conferences

I'm a big believer in dealer education, and the state dealer organizations are some of the best places to find critical information. I encourage our clients to be members because the state organizations have their fingers on the pulse of what's impacting its dealers, from legislation to litigation and a whole bunch of practical business issues like inventory, employee issues and more. Many of these organizations hold their annual conferences in the summer, so take advantage and make plans to attend yours. Take advantage of the networking opportunities and meet other dealers and third party service providers that can help your business.

When you get back to the office, share the information you learned. Have a brown bag lunch session with your team, distribute materials that you bring back, and make sure your folks get the benefit of this knowledge.

September's Focus is on Training

For September, I challenge you to ask yourself another hard question: am I providing my employees with the tools and information they need to be successful? A demonstrable training strategy will not only help protect your business by ensuring that your team is handling issues the right way, but it will make a great impression on any capital provider or regulator that takes a look. Examine each function of your business and ask yourself whether there is sufficient training in this area. Then turn your attention to more global issues like prevention of identity theft, information security, anti-harassment and other human resources type issues, and fill in any gaps that exist. Education is a passion of mine, which is why Ignite's Training Unleashed online portal provides our industry specific classes at a low monthly cost. We've made great training simple and cheap. Email info@IgniteCP.com for more information.

October - It's never too early to focus on End of Year Issues.

Every December, I seem to get hit with lots of questions about related finance companies, discounts, 1099-c issues, whether to sell notes or not, and other end of year concerns. Don't wait until the holiday crush to ask these questions. Pencil in a few hours this month to get with your accountant and walk through your end of year plans. It will save you lots of stress later and you may be able to identify some strategies that will save on your tax bill.

November - Be Thankful that your Credit Furnishing and Dispute Handling House is in Order

The most common lawsuit brought against creditors concerns their credit furnishing and dispute handling obligations. Do you have the needed policy content to protect your business on these issues? Is your staff adequately trained? Are mini-audits being conducted throughout the year to help identify any gaps or concerns? Are direct disputes responded to in a timely and sufficient way? This is the month to turn your attention to this subject and investigate whether your resources are adequate. Hopefully you've identified any needs during your policy and training initiatives, but if you're still lacking now is the time to make the fix.

December - Finish the Year Strong!

Time flies when you're having fun. Has it been a year already? If you've done all of the things we've discussed, you're in a great position and have taken great steps to protect your business. Now I want you to finish the year with two things that aren't usually thought about as compliance subjects.

First, since insurance policy renewals tend to happen later in the year, do a review of your various insurance policies. Garage liability is great, but it's not nearly sufficient to cover all the risks faced by an independent dealer or finance company. Do you have Errors and Omissions coverage to protect against errors such as mathematical and calculation mistakes, failing to send a statutory required notice letter, orother behavior that leads to a lawsuit? I highly recommend this type of coverage. Yes, it can be expensive, but that can be offset with a high deductible, think of it as catastrophic coverage. Two other types of insurance to consider are ransomware coverage and data breach coverage. The costs that result from these types of actions can be catastrophic, so it's worthwhile to ask your agent about these types of policies.

Finally, when was the last time you had your Employee Handbook reviewed? It's important that the rules of the employment relationship are established in writing with your personnel. Have your content reviewed and go into the New Year with confidence that you are protected in this critical area.

Conclusions

There you have it, a "trip around the sun" strategy to protect your business in about 2,000 words. By following the methodology I've set out you'll be well on your way to achieving impactful results in 2022! Space constraints didn't allow me to do a deep dive into each of these important subjects, but I've written about all of them in the past, so feel free to search Google with my name and any of these topics and I bet you'll find a relevant article to provide more guidance. As always, be sure to email me if you have specific questions, would like to address any of the information in more detail, or have suggestions for future articles. I hope everyone has a great Holiday season, a strong End of Year, and a great start to 2022.

CHAPTER SEVEN

Bonus Content

I've collected some amusing stories along the way, and I told myself if I ever wrote a book there would have to be room for this material. These gems didn't fit in well with the previous chapters, but much like outtakes and bloopers in the closing credits, I included these here for your lighthearted enjoyment.

"SIR..... THIS IS DISCRIMINATION

I had recently left the law firm where I had begun handling litigation, having opened my own modest office, which consisted of an office desk, two chairs, a file cabinet, and a receptionist's desk. Truth be told, I didn't have a receptionist and had no use for the desk, but it was my wife's and we didn't have room to store it in our small house.

I had a lot of free time in those days, I had just left the firm and the phone wasn't exactly ringing off the hook, so when it did ring, I excitedly listened. A gentleman called me and said he saw my street sign and wanted to come in to discuss a "slam dunk case of discrimination against the police". I had never handled a discrimination case before, but I figured maybe the facts were good enough to make it worth my while, so I began asking him questions.

He explained that he had met a female acquaintance at a bar and one thing led to another, so he went and rented a hotel room. He and his female friend spent a few hours together, but pretty soon they were out of alcohol. He offered to go out and pick some up, but his friend, using her feminine wares, encouraged him to stay put, saying she could call her brother and they'd send him to pick up some booze. The kid shows up, he gives the kid his car keys, and off the kid supposedly goes to get their beverage of choice. Ten minutes go by, twenty minutes go by, a half an hour goes by, and the kid never comes back. Expressing concern, the female friend says she's going to look in the parking lot and make sure her brother isn't out there. Not shockingly, she disappears, never to be heard from again.

My potential new client tells me he was pretty quick to figure out he'd been scammed (yes, I'm serious, he said he was pretty quick) and the genius calls the police. Low and behold, the police come to the hotel, hear his story, and arrest him for solicitation of prostitution, plus a charge for the small amount of marijuana they found on him. After listening patiently, I simply ask "so where's the part about discrimination?" Non-plussed, he shouts at me "SIR, my car was stolen, I call the police, and they come and arrest me, if that's not discrimination I don't know what is." I told him that perhaps he needed a lawyer more familiar with discrimination matters and got him off the phone.

"I'M NOT EVEN QUALIFIED TO WORK AT MCDONALDS"

I had dabbled in a few minor personal injury cases while at the law firm, plus I handled some insurance defense work involving car accidents, so when a lawyer I knew told me he was going to work for a company and needed to get some of his cases covered, I gladly took a slip and fall case representing a lady named Brenda. This was in the days prior to tort reform in Texas, and plaintiffs' lawyers pulled down good money, so I had dollar signs dancing in my head and figured I'd get the case ready for trial and the insurance company would offer a settlement.

The problem with personal injury cases like this was that you worked completely on contingency, meaning you didn't recover any money unless the case settled or you won at trial. Plus, the lawyer was responsible for obtaining medical records, taking depositions, and paying for the myriad of other expenses that could come up preparing the case. Undeterred, I thought this was my chance to begin a career working some personal injury cases into my practice. Lot's of attorney's did it, how hard could it be?

Brenda was a nurse prior to her slip and fall, and after her accident she was unable to work due to damage in her back. Her medical records clearly showed she suffered an injury, and the treating physician produced a report that supported her case. She attended physical therapy and had good records to document she was doing all she could to aid her recovery, and her income had been obviously reduced because she couldn't do the lifting and other physical labor that her nursing jobs required.

My only concern about the case was that she hadn't worked in over a year, and had made no effort to find employment. I understood she couldn't work on her feet or do the labor she previously had, but I thought that it was a weakness in her case that she hadn't made an effort to mitigate the economic damages and I told her this as we prepared for her deposition. She looked at me and said "I started as a nurse's assistant when I was 17 and then went to school and became a nurse, I've done this my whole life, I don't know how to do anything else, I've never done anything else, I'm not even qualified to work at McDonalds". Feeling sympathy for her, I let the issue drop.

I had already invested a few thousand dollars in expenses in her case, so her deposition was a critical event. If she did well, I thought the insurance company would put a respectable settlement offer on the table. The day of her deposition arrives, she gets sworn in, and she's doing very well answering the insurance lawyer's questions about the slip and fall, her injuries, and her recovery efforts.

The subject of her job history comes up and the lawyer starts questioning her about her nursing jobs prior to the accident, and works his way backwards asking her about her various jobs over the past two decades. When he gets to high school, he starts asking her whether she worked and she answers that from 10th grade until she graduated she worked AT MCDONALDS. She had been a cashier, she had been a cook, she worked the take out line, she'd done basically everything one can do working fast food. I was crestfallen. The thing I told her I was worried about, her failure to mitigate any economic damages, was now the issue he was pounding her on, relentlessly questioning her about her failure to look for any job in over a year.

What made things worse, though, was that she had lied to me. She said she wasn't qualified to do anything, not even work at a McDonalds, yet she had done just that for over 2 years in high school. Handling a case like this means you are betting your own time and money on the outcome, so you'd better have honesty and trust with your client. After her performance, we had neither and I couldn't represent her anymore. She had lied to me, I felt she didn't care, and certainly wasn't going to throw good money after bad and continue to put money into her case. I withdrew from representing her and told her to find another lawyer. I don't even know how the case ever turned out.

And that was the start, and end, of my life as a high flying personal injury lawyer.

MY WORST DEPOSITION

My car dealer client and its related finance company had been sued over what was alleged to be a wrongful repossession. The dispute surrounded whether some payments were made and whether my client had provided an extension and also included the collection practices used. This was back before dealer management software systems were as fancy as they are now, back when dealers still used hand receipts, ledger books, and other prehistoric tools.

The key witness for my client was a rather colorful character. He liked to play things fast and loose. For instance, he was great at imitating voices, so when he had a customer on the phone he'd be speaking as the collector, then ask the customer to hold while he got his manager, then he'd get back on the phone and disguise his voice and would have a conversation as "the manager". Of course, I only found these morsels out later. At the time, I was just concerned about the case at hand and preparing him adequately for what I anticipated would be a lively examination.

We spent hours together. I walked him through every nuance of the case. I explained the plaintiff's claims, our defenses, the key facts in dispute, and how it all fit together with the law. I was impressed with my thorough preparation and was confident that I put him through questioning as every bit rigorous as he would experience in the witness chair during his deposition.

The day came and the festivities began. My opposing counsel, who was a bit of a hot head with a reputation for intimidation, began his questioning.

“Please State your name”.

“Joe Smith, I mean Joe Johnson”, the witness replied(I’ve changed the names for the sake of privacy).

The lawyer looked at the witness and asked “Which is it, Joe Smith or Joe Johnson?”

“Well, that’s a good question”, the witness answered. I’m Joe Smith to my parents, and I’m Joe Smith at work, but when I talk to customers I’m Joe Johnson”.

“So your real name is Joe Smith, and that’s what you go by at work, unless you talk to customers, then you’re Joe Johnson, is that correct?” he asked.

“Well no, because I use a few other names too, just depending on the situation”.

“Okay”, the lawyer continues, “let’s revisit the issue of your name later, where do you live?”

“123 Sycamore Lane”, my witness responds. “No, that’s not right, I moved from there, now I’m at 456 Jones Street. Well, I don’t sleep there though, now I’m at.......

By now, the lawyer is red-faced, turns in my direction and says “You son of a $*&, you did this, you coached him to be evasive”. He gets up, fists balled, glaring at me, and then challenges me, “Let’s take this outside”. Knowing that the court reporter was catching every word, I stated that for the record, opposing counsel jumped from his seat with fists raised and made an aggressive move towards me, and told him that the deposition was over and he'd better leave the office before I filed a motion for sanctions. I may or may not have said I'd gladly kick his %&^.

Like I said, this was my worst deposition ever. Worst lawyering on my part, too. I prepared him for every question I could think of except the two guaranteed questions that start every deposition, "what's your name and where do you live." Needless to say, from then on, whenever I prepped a witness, those were the first two questions I asked.

"ARE YOU AN ALIEN"? MY FAVORITE DEPOSITION STORY

The combination of auto finance and lawsuits has certainly taken me to some interesting places. After about five years of representing my first client's dealership, he started a finance company that was an indirect lender, meaning it purchased contracts originated by other dealers. It enjoyed success and expanded its dealer base nationally. As it grew, so did my colorful experiences, and the story I'm about to share has lived on in infamy for twenty-five years.

The finance company had purchased a contract from a dealer in Rosewell, New Mexico. Shortly after, the consumer filed a lawsuit due to some issue with the car, and the consumer's lawyer, following the "more pockets is better" approach, sued the finance company too because it held the contract. This led to the dealership and finance company filing cross-claims against each other, so we were at odds not only with the plaintiff, but with the other defendant.

Early on, it was pretty clear that the dealer just needed to settle the case, but unfortunately it was being represented by attorney's hired by its insurance company and insurance company lawyers, in my experience, like to work a file to death before exploring settlement. After some initial requests for documents and interrogatories, it was time for depositions, and since the case was filed in New Mexico, we had to go to Roswell.

The other defendant even asking to take the deposition of our corporate representative was a nuisance move just to inconvenience us, since we knew nothing about the dealings in the underlying transaction and our dealer agreement was clear on indemnity. We had to produce a witness, though, so myself and my client flew out to Roswell, New Mexico. This client was born and raised in New York just like me, and he was even more of a pushy and aggressive New Yorker than I was. We were ticked off and in a bad mood before we even landed.

Our spirits improved as we discovered that Roswell's claim to fame was that it was the location of a supposed flying saucer landing in the late 1940's and the town catered to conspiracy theorists and tourists interested in unidentified flying objects and extra-terrestrial life. Since we flew in the day before the deposition to meet with our local counsel for dinner, we had a few hours to kill and visited the UFO Museum and some other alien-themed venues. Quite unexpectedly, we were enjoying ourselves.

Our moods reverted back to poor the following day, when the depositions began. We sat through the testimony of the plaintiff and the dealer and now it was my client's turn.

Because there were three parties and the two defendants had claims against the other, both the attorney representing the plaintiff and the dealer got to question him. The plaintiff's lawyer was young, about my age, and did a respectable job of questioning my witness. He was more concerned with establishing for the record that my client had no information that would contradict the claims being made by the plaintiff. He stuck to the basic facts and was efficient in his questioning, which was appreciated since we had a late plane to catch.

Things went south in a hurry when it was the dealer's lawyer's time to ask questions. I had spent some time handling insurance defense cases in my early career at a law firm, and I knew the games that were played, so I didn't expect this to go smoothly. It didn't help that this particular attorney was confrontational, brash, and at five and a half feet tall and just as wide, resembled a fire hydrant when his face flushed as he got angry.

He immediately moved to "mark his territory", firing away questions in rapid fashion, trying to take control of the room. Knowing my client as well as I did, I knew he'd respond in a similar fashion, so in an effort to slow down the tempo, every few questions I'd whisper in his ear, trying to break the flow of questions and keep his temper in check.

My efforts weren't appreciated by the defense lawyer. I was only supposed to be an observer at these depositions. I wasn't licensed to practice in New Mexico and couldn't represent the company in the proceedings. I was in attendance because I managed all of the client's litigation nationwide and had been the one to hire the local attorney that was actually defending the deposition.

I should mention that different jurisdictions have different procedural rules. In Texas, at the time, it was permissible for the witness's attorney to converse with the witness during a deposition. In New Mexico, though, it was improper, so after about the fifth time of whispering, the fire hydrant of a lawyer got mad, his neck and face turning red in stark contrast to his white shirt. He admonished me for my behavior and scolded me not to speak to the witness again. I looked to our counsel, a tall, gangly and timid gentleman who looked like he'd be more comfortable doing research in a library than as a litigator, and he simply shrugged in agreement. Not in the mood to back down, though, I continued the whispering a few more times, just to see how far I could knock the defense lawyer off of his game.

Up to this point, my client was enjoying the sparring, but now he didn't want to miss out on the fun. Midway through the next question he blurts out a question of his own. "Are you an alien"? The defense lawyer looked at him confused, unsure what joke he had missed, and continued with his question. Undeterred, my client asked again "I'm serious, are you an alien"? The defense lawyer again turned a deep shade of red, banged the table, and shouted "Do you think this is funny"?, to which my client responded "I'm being serious, there's an exhibit at the UFO museum about how aliens can be living among us, and I want to know whether an alien is taking my deposition". I glanced over at our local counsel, who looked like he was going to pass out.

Looking to get control of the witness, the defense lawyer said "I get to ask the questions here and you need to get serious". To which my client retorted "Are you refusing to answer the question because you are an alien"? It was all downhill from there; the defense lawyer literally turned fire hydrant red, our lawyer buried his face in his hands, speechless, and I whispered in my client's ear that he'd better not pull this same stunt at the sanctions hearing that I was certain was coming.

Miraculously, the deposition ended without a fist fight, we finished in time to make our return flight, the case settled a few weeks later, and we never had to return to Roswell. To top it off, we had a great story to tell, and tell it we have, countless times over the years. Oh, and about ten year's later I again had the need for local representation in New Mexico and I looked up our attorney. Not surprisingly, he remembered me. Also not surprisingly, he no longer handled litigation and didn't take the case.

Made in the USA
Monee, IL
04 November 2026

67384095R00148